"The period of time between middle age and old age has not yet been given a name, but with characteristic wisdom, warmth and insight, Christopher Ash has provided us with a navigational map to chart our progress. The unique privileges, challenges and opportunities of this era are to be enjoyed rather than endured as we follow Jesus and seek to make a difference for his kingdom."

Alistair Begg, Bible Teacher, Truth For Life;
Senior Pastor, Parkside Church, Cleveland, OH

"In our fifties and sixties it can be so easy, so comfortable, to step back from serving in the church, stop getting involved in the lives of needy people, and simply settle into a comfortable spirituality that lacks passion for prayer and for new discoveries in the Bible. In this book, Christopher Ash kindly nudges us out of complacency, encouraging us to steward this particular season of life for the kingdom of God."

Nancy Guthrie, Sixty-something Author and Bible Teacher

"This book is a lifebuoy to lift you out of the 'Sea of Disappointment' and put you on the 'Path of Contentment' as you navigate your fifties and sixties. But whatever your age, you will be steadied and strengthened by this pastoral gem from Christopher Ash. I found myself face to face with familiar griefs but also such comforting remedies. The lies we breathe are destabilising us—here is real stabilising truth and love."

Simon Manchester, Retired Minister,
St Thomas' North Sydney, Australia

"I wasn't aware that I needed this, but Christopher has written a profoundly helpful challenge to take up the cross of Christ in our fifties and sixties rather than settle into a duvet of comfort or drift into a pattern of complaint. It's all delivered with the warmth of a friend—typical of Christopher's writing—and did me much good."

Matt Fuller, Senior Minister,
Christ Church Mayfair, London, UK

Not Old, *not young,* **Not Done.**

Following Jesus in Your 50s & 60s

Christopher Ash

Not Old, Not Young, Not Done

Published by:
The Good Book Company

thegoodbook.com | thegoodbook.co.uk
thegoodbook.com.au | thegoodbook.co.nz

Design by André Parker

ISBN: 9781802543254 | JOB-008257 | Printed in India

Contents

"So, it's your fiftieth birthday on Saturday. Congratulations! I hope you'll be celebrating." Michael wasn't so sure. Thirty had felt grown up and cheerful; he had enjoyed a lively party then. Forty? Well, that felt a little ambiguous; the celebrations were more muted. But fifty? The kind comment that "fifty is the new forty" only went so far. It did feel like a bit of a watershed. It was as though the morning of his life had moved into the afternoon.

Introduction

The Afternoon of Life

When the days drew near for [Jesus] to be taken up, he set his face to go to Jerusalem. …

Yet another said, "I will follow you, Lord, but … " Jesus said to him, "No one who puts his hand to the plough and looks back is fit for the kingdom of God."

Luke 9:51, 61-62

However you feel about having turned fifty and however many years have passed since, I write to wish you a good afternoon of your life.

Let me explain what I mean. Very roughly, by "the afternoon of life" I mean your fifties and sixties—two decades when you might sense that you are entering or have entered a new season. I want to encourage you who have put your hand to the plough in the service of

Jesus not to look back but to walk on faithfully through this window of your life. As you follow the Lord Jesus, may you be one who sets your face to finish the course the Father has set before you. May God bless you in the afternoon of your life and make you a faithful follower of Jesus.

Not Old, Not Young...

I began this little book shortly before I turned seventy. (And that's another milestone—perhaps a story for a future day.) I can't remember exactly when a friend suggested jotting down some pastoral thoughts about our fifties and sixties. But anyway, just as I leave that window of life behind, here are those thoughts. In most of the world today and for the larger part of human history, your fifties and sixties would be the evening of life. You would not be surprised to die during those decades. But largely, in prosperous, Western societies with nourishing diets, good health care and long life-expectancy, the evening is often postponed until our seventies, or perhaps even our eighties or nineties.

What we are left with is this fascinatingly ambiguous time in between younger middle age and old age. You are not old, but you are not young. For simplicity I call this our fifties and sixties although, of course, you may perhaps feel that it began earlier or, more likely, that it is lasting longer (as people like me in our early seventies rather like to hope).

What I have in mind is some mix of the following characteristics. Here are six markers for "the afternoon of life". I realise that for every characteristic I propose there will be a hundred exceptions. Each of our lives is different from every other. And yet I think the picture I am about to paint is recognisable.

MARKER 1: CHILDREN LEAVING HOME

My first marker is that your children are beginning to leave home. If you have children, that is. But, even if you don't, this is a stage of life in which your married contemporaries with children are seeing them begin perhaps to start an apprenticeship, to go to college or university, to get a job, to leave home. The days of nappies and diapers are long past. Memories of pre-school or kindergarten are distant. The years of waiting at the end of the day at the school gate have ended. The routine of the youngster taking the bus to high school is no longer a part of family life. You are in new territory. Of course, social trends towards later marriage and sometimes much later childbearing may change significantly the age at which this happens—and housing costs may mean that we have adult children living with us well into their 20s. But the time comes when children are no longer at home, or at least no longer under our authority.

MARKER 2: CARE FOR ELDERLY PARENTS

Along with children leaving home comes—for many—a growing responsibility to care for one or more ageing parents. The days when your parents were net givers to the ecology of your life are fading. They used to have energy, money and perhaps time to help. But they are growing older. Instead of tripping up, they now speak of "having a fall". Grievous medical diagnoses become more common. Bereavement strikes. Rather than looking after you, they need more and more care. Perhaps a significant burden of this falls upon you. You may belong, as the saying goes, to "the sandwich generation", squeezed between care for the older generation and responsibilities towards younger ones.

MARKER 3: AN EASING OF MONEY WORRIES

My third marker is a lessening of money worries. Not for all, of course, for there are a hundred and one reasons why many experience financial pressure as never before in the afternoon of life. But for many of us, as the expense of raising children comes to an end, there is some easing of concerns about money. For some, the death of a parent brings a significant inheritance which places this third marker on steroids.

MARKER 4: FAMILIARITY WITH OUR JOBS

My fourth marker is that stage of employment in which we are generally familiar with our work. These can be years in which we are generally confident that we can do our jobs, and do them pretty well. We may even be at the top of our game. We have been engaged in our occupations for more than a couple of decades and have developed a certain level of skill. We may even be quite senior in our fields. The prospect of retirement comes into view and perhaps the possibility of taking early retirement. At the very least, we begin to think about these things.

Once again, there are many exceptions. For some, this is a stage of disappointment, boredom and disillusion with a working life that feels frustrating or wasted. But, at the very least, many of us have got used to what we have been doing.

MARKER 5: GOOD HEALTH

Along with all this, there may be a continuation of generally robust health. Even to say this will cause pain to those for whom the opposite is true and for whom the evening has come early—perhaps much earlier than we expected or hoped. For some, this stage of life coincides with a terrible medical diagnosis or the onset of a progressive disease that slows life almost to a halt. And of course, some will die long before there is anything that can be thought of as a quiet evening of life.

But many of us—at least for some years—still enjoy steady good health. Perhaps, as our afternoon continues, we find ourselves with a little less energy and a few more niggles. Yet we can still exercise, play sport, travel, enjoy the delights of intimacy in marriage and be thankful for many of the physical blessings of this life.

MARKER 6: MORE TIME

My final marker is that many of us have more time at our disposal. It may not feel like it in our frenetic and distracted cultures. But the truth is that the incessant demands of a young family are over and the stresses of proving ourselves in a new job are a thing of the past. We may still be wildly busy—and even pride ourselves on being so—and yet we have more choices in our use of time.

Not Done

I hope this gives a feel for what I mean by "the afternoon of life". There are other markers I might have developed. We begin to be targeted by ads for holidays for more senior people, with models who try to make us think we are much younger than we are. People try to sell us better reading lights, more sophisticated hearing aids, and many other things we perhaps think we are not yet ready for!

I have been prompted to write this book because I am not aware of very much Christian writing that addresses this in-between time of life. There are some excellent and enormously wise and helpful books about old age, and I warmly commend these.[1] There are resources for teenagers, young singles, older singles, young marrieds, and parents of young children and teenagers. But, unless I am mistaken, there is not much that speaks to these in-between years, which are for many of us a distinctive period both of spiritual danger and spiritual opportunity. A pastor friend of mine says that this point in our lives is often a fork in the road of discipleship; it may lead to decades of exceptional fruitfulness or develop into sadly wasted years. If he is right, it is important to choose carefully. So, if you recognise yourself in at least some of my six markers, this book may be for you.

---

1 I have particularly appreciated Derek Prime, *A Good Old Age* and J.I.Packer, *Finishing our Course with Joy* (each printed in a reassuringly large font!).

It is worth saying that—as I leave behind this stage of life and the evening beckons—I am not here describing all the things I have done. Far from it. More often than not, I have written the book I wish someone had given me before my fiftieth birthday. Perhaps it might have saved me from some of my many failures and mistakes had I been humble enough to read it. I hope it will do you good.

One of the challenges of writing a pastoral book like this is knowing how much to dig deep into practical questions. Because our lives and circumstances are so wildly different, I have tended to err on the side of speaking to the heart rather than seeking to offer practical counsel.

At a stage of life in which positives and negatives, joys and challenges, jostle with one another in what can feel like a confusing jumble, I write to help you think things out in the light of God's truth. I write to wish you God's blessing, God's keeping, God's face shining on you, God being gracious to you, God giving you peace in this window of your life. If God is your Father through Jesus, then you may say with David that every one of your days were written in God's book before one of them dawned (Psalm 139:16). I want to wish you rich blessings in each one of those days. I hope to think with you about what that means and what it is to be a glad disciple of Jesus in these particular days. You are not old, not young, and most certainly *not done* in your service of, and growth in, the Lord. I hope you will be a man or woman who knows through these years the joy, the peace, the purpose and the contentment that Jesus offers to his followers. That you will hear on the last day those wonderful words: "Well done, good and faithful servant" (Matthew 25:21).

Questions and Responses

1. Does this "afternoon" idea in any way fit you at your stage of life? Which, if any, of these six markers describe you?

2. Are there any ways in which you are conscious of being in days of important choices, facing a fork in the road of your life?

At the funeral of an older member of his church, Gary had the opportunity to catch up with two former members, both now in their early sixties, who had travelled from different parts of the country to be there. He had known each of them well and remembered them as zealous, prayerful, energetic, and courageous disciples of Jesus. They had been a joy to have as members of the church. Dalip's work had taken him to another part of the country where he married and had children. Amani also married and moved to where her husband worked; they too had children.

But as they chatted, Gary could not help being struck by the difference between them. Outwardly all seemed well with both, in their marriages, their families, their jobs and their health. But inwardly, what a contrast! Amani was as eager to grow in the knowledge of God as when she had been in her twenties. She talked still about her love for Jesus, her hunger for the Scriptures, her zeal for the gospel. There was a warmth of maturity now, and there were scars of sadnesses. There were grey hairs but a fresh and zealous heart. But with Dalip—oh, it was so sad—all the talk was about his career, his successes, his family, his house. There were not so many grey hairs, but there was a grey heart.

Chapter 1

A Wise Heart

Keep your heart with all vigilance, for from it flow the springs of life.

Proverbs 4:23

This chapter focuses on the heart. I don't know if you can identify with Dalip or with Amani, or perhaps with a bit of both. I want to think with you about your heart before we dive into chapters focusing on particular challenges and issues, because the heart drives how we respond to each of those.

The heart is at the core of your being. It shapes your affections and your aversions (what you want and what you hate); out of its abundance you speak (Luke 6:45), and from its depths you act. Above all, life springs from it. Therefore keep your heart, writes Solomon, with all vigilance (Proverbs 4:23).

But—as we know too well in painful experience—with Adam's sin, our hearts fell from this beauty and purity.

Every affection became tainted, each thought spoiled, word after word less than pure, deed after deed twisted and full of iniquity. God "saw that the wickedness of man was great in the earth, and that every intention of the thoughts of his heart was only evil continually" (Genesis 6:5). The heart became something deeply deceitful, so that we deceive ourselves about our motives; it developed a desperate sickness, so that out of it sprang death rather than life (Jeremiah 17:9). For out of our hearts come "evil thoughts, sexual immorality, theft, murder, adultery, coveting, wickedness, deceit, sensuality, envy, slander, pride, foolishness" (Mark 7:21-22).

How precious therefore are the promises of the new covenant: that the good and perfect law of God will be written on the heart, so that we begin not only to do it but to desire to do it (Jeremiah 31:33), so that a hard heart of stone becomes a soft heart of flesh, a new heart in which the Holy Spirit makes his dwelling (Ezekiel 36:26). How wonderful to be gradually conformed to the image of God's Son in our hearts (Romans 8:29).

So, as we think about the afternoon of life, I want to exhort us to seek afresh a pure heart and a wise heart, and to be vigilant during these years in keeping it with care.

Pray Afresh for a Pure Heart

Blessed are the pure in heart, for they shall see God.
(Matthew 5:8)

Let the words of my mouth and the meditation of my heart

be acceptable in your sight,
O Lord, my rock and my redeemer. (Psalm 19:14)

What David prays in Psalm 19, Jesus would no doubt often have prayed during his life on earth. You and I ought to pray this also—to cry out in prayer that even the hidden meditation of my heart will be pure in God's sight. For none of the more seemingly "practical" matters treated later in this book will be worth anything without a pure heart. Uprightness of heart is foundational to the life of faith, for God saves "the upright in heart" (Psalm 7:10). Only the one with "clean hands" (actions) and "a pure heart" (motivations) has the right to dwell in the presence of God (Psalm 24:3-4). Jesus is this man. His purity of heart is given to us by grace through faith. But it must then begin to grow in us as the Holy Spirit makes us more like Jesus.

Nothing will frighten us more than the thought that we might begin well but prove in the end to have a hardened heart, a seared conscience (1 Timothy 4:2) or a heart rendered fruitless by sin (see Matthew 13:22). And we will fear hypocrisy. So much of Jesus' rebuke was targeted at hypocrisy, the mask that conceals the heart with superficially righteous words or actions (e.g. Matthew 23:13-29).

We must be realistic about the deceptiveness of sin. For the human heart "is deceitful above all things, and desperately sick" (Jeremiah 17:9). Like those about whom Paul writes in 2 Timothy, we may not only deceive others by our hypocrisy, but fool ourselves into thinking we are inwardly healthy (2 Timothy 3:13—"deceiving and being deceived"). Like David, and like Jesus on earth, we will pray, "Prove me, O Lord, and try me; test my heart and my mind" (Psalm 26:2). Ask God to search your heart afresh at this stage of life, to shine the light of his Spirit into the dark corners, to see what weeds may have grown unnoticed over the years.

One diagnostic question is this: what do I deeply want, desire and love? Perhaps this shows itself when my mind is like a manual gearbox in "neutral", not consciously thinking about anything in particular. To what are my desires drawn by the hidden magnet of my heart? A related question is to ask is: what do I most profoundly hate and fear? What worries keep me awake at night? From what possible futures do I recoil in dread?

As you examine your heart there will be plenty of reason to move to confession and repentance. No self-reflection will be complete without a fresh repentance. So let me encourage you now to bring what you have found into the light of God's truth. You know that God will not despise a broken and a contrite heart (Psalm 51:17), so bring yours to him with confidence in his love and forgiveness. In particular, seek God's grace to repent again from disordered affections. You may have found in yourself lukewarm desires for the things of God and warm passions for things hateful to God. Cry afresh for God to warm the former and freeze out the latter. Take time to confess sin at this window of life. Resolve to walk through the afternoon of your life with a clear conscience (Acts 24:16).[2]

---

2 See my little book *Pure Joy: Rediscover Your Conscience* (IVP UK, 2012).

Seek Afresh a Wise Heart

The teaching of the wise is a fountain of life,
that one may turn away from the snares of death.
(Proverbs 13:14)

As well as a pure heart, pray to learn wisdom. We ought to walk in wisdom at every stage of life, to look carefully to how we walk, not as unwise but as wise (Ephesians 5:15). But there are at least two blessings attached to wisdom in the afternoon of life.

WISDOM CAN GROW AS OTHER THINGS FADE

Even in your fifties, you have probably become aware that your mental agility has dropped, your memory has grown less acute, and your ability to think laterally or quickly has deteriorated. You are, quite simply, less quick on your (mental) feet. Why then, we may ask, is human leadership in the Bible vested in elders? Why not entrust leadership to "youngers", who have more energy and more fleetness of foot in their thinking? The answer is that an older man or woman who has been sitting at the feet of Christ will have learned a measure of wisdom. Often there is a fountain of life here that may not be found in the words of a younger person. Many faculties fade, but wisdom can grow and grow.

WISDOM POINTS FORWARD TO FINAL SALVATION

A second blessing is that wisdom is like a stream that flows all the way to our final salvation, like a river of hopefulness leading to a sea of joy. The Scriptures make us "wise for salvation" (2 Timothy 3:15). This is a thought-provoking phrase. It implies that salvation, although begun now as we belong to Christ, will not be completed until the final day. And it means that wisdom is a means God uses to lead us on that river or path that ends with final salvation. Wisdom is therefore pregnant with hope.

Growing in Wisdom

One of the distinctions I have noticed among elderly Christians is this. Some, even in their seventies and eighties, seem to remain fresh in their walk with God. They appear always to be learning, growing, thinking, pondering. You never get the impression that they feel they know enough or understand sufficiently. And yet others somehow begin to "smell" a bit stale. It is not simply that they sometimes retell the same stories and repeat the same things; I guess we all do that as we age ("Oh no, Dad! Not that story again!"). Rather it is that their grasp of the Scriptures and their understanding of the gospel seem frozen in time, in some earlier stage of their lives. They hark back to some teacher or preacher by whom they were blessed more than they reach forwards in seeking a deeper understanding. Not that there is anything wrong with looking back in gratitude to one or another who has helped shape our Christian lives. But with some, the predominant impression is a looking back much more than a reaching forward.

If that distinction is visible in older age, the seeds are often sown in the afternoon of life. Let me therefore encourage you to be intentional in growing in godly wisdom. How might you do this?

1. REFRESH YOUR PERSONAL DEVOTIONS

First, you will plan carefully that your personal devotional Bible reading will be more than a superficial series of hurried reminders of what you already know. You will find ways to engage more deeply with a Bible book or theme, to grapple afresh with it, to make some notes about it and just simply to spend time thinking and meditating on it. I know in my experience that there are seasons when my devotional reading, morning by morning, is dry, shallow and frustratingly lacking in spiritual nutrition. That may happen because of sickness or exhaustion; it sometimes coincides with overwhelming busyness. It is perhaps a necessary part of the life of faith that we persevere through such times and persist in reading our Bibles day by day. And then there are other times when a Bible book just comes alive and speaks to us afresh morning by morning. We find ourselves talking to others about it, pondering it at odd moments during the day, feeding on fresh wonders in God's word. Let us pray and do all we can to give space for such times of growth and depth.

2. READ NOURISHING CHRISTIAN WRITING

Second, I want to suggest that you take care to read nourishing Christian writings. Much that is called Christian literature is—to be brutally honest—little more than ephemeral fluff. (Perhaps you will think this book is one such example, although I hope not.) If it's within your capabilities, seek to develop a pattern of reading in which you deliberately read meatier writings. Often that will mean mining the rich veins of biblical ore in some of the older writers. At the moment I am reading slowly through John Calvin's *Institutes of the Christian Religion*, which is one of the classics of Christian thinking in the age of the Reformation. Often I read just three or four pages in a day and make a few notes. But the cumulative experience is profoundly nourishing. It forces me to think harder than I otherwise would about God—Father, Son, and Holy Spirit—about what it is to be human, about salvation, and so on. And, as I do, I hope I grow in understanding.

Why not be brave and read some of the Church Fathers: the great church leaders of the first five or so centuries whose writings laid so many foundations for our Christian thinking (Augustine's *Confessions*, for example)? Our church pastor has suggested we read Athanasius' *On the Incarnation* over the next few weeks. Delve into Martin Luther and other Reformers from the 16th century (for example, Luther's *The Bondage of the Will*). Dip or dive into the Puritans from the 17th century (for example, Richard Sibbes' *The Bruised Reed*). Read some good Christian biographies (for example, Iain Murray on Martyn Lloyd-Jones or Ellen Vaughn on Elisabeth Elliot). I remember reading George Marsden's biography of the 18th-century preacher Jonathan Edwards and learning so much.

3. DEVELOP INTENTIONAL CHRISTIAN FRIENDSHIPS

Third, you will want—insofar as you are able—to develop the kinds of Christian friendships in which you can have substantial discussions about the Scriptures and the gospel. You could seek out friends who will form with you a book group to meet once a month and read through a good Christian book. Many have found this richly rewarding. Or ask a friend who has read a nourishing book to share some of it with you. Or simply read the Bible together, share your reflections and pray. Time spent listening to brothers and sisters in Christ is not wasted. So often their words can shine light into our blind spots, and their experience can enrich our grasp of the wonder and grace of God.

4. KEEP A JOURNAL OF THE LIFE OF FAITH

Fourth—and in a way, this is where we begin to move towards the heart of wisdom—develop a life of faith in which you seek to walk with God "through all the changing scenes of life". Many have found it helpful to keep a notebook or journal in which you record something of your life of faith and reflect on what is happening to you and in you. If you do this, try to include what the Puritans called "heart work", focusing not simply on externals but probing deeper into what is going on inside you. It is possible to become morbidly introspective, but I suspect that, for many of us, the danger is the opposite: that we take too little time to work on our hearts, our desires, our affections, our delights, our hopes and our fears. What is God teaching you in this season of life? How is he shaping you to become more like Jesus? Of course, the self-deception of our hearts is so deep that our answers can never be more than approximate and provisional. But ask for God's help in this, and he will give you insight into your own heart.

In all these ways and more, do what you can to grow in wisdom, to guard your heart and to make sure that you do not waste this precious season of your life. Nothing is more important than your heart. Watch over it with care!

Questions and Responses

1. Have you taken time quietly to ponder, reflect, and act on the Scriptures in this chapter? If not, why not go back and choose one verse and Bible truth on which to meditate, and then turn it into prayer?

2. Of what sins have you felt the need specifically to repent afresh? You may find it helpful to share this with a partner in prayer.

3. How healthy is your regular pattern of personal prayer and Bible reading? Are there ways in which you can refresh this?

4. What nourishing Christian book might you study? If in doubt, ask your pastor or minister for advice!

5. Review your Christian friendships. Are there ways in which you could be more intentional with your friends to encourage one another to grow in wisdom?

6. How much do you think about and review your life of faith? Are there ways in which you can do this that avoid morbid introspection but encourage you towards hope-filled wisdom?

Gareth and Dave were in their mid-sixties, chatting on the sideline as they watched their grandchildren in a football (aka soccer) match.

"I used to play quite a bit," said Gareth, "but now I struggle even to walk very far. It's my hip. I hope they can fix it soon with a replacement. There seem to be more and more things about me that need fixing. Still, they seem to be able to fix most things nowadays."

"Oh, sure," smiled Dave. "I hope you get that hip replacement soon. It's great what they can fix. But I wish my cousin's health could be fixed like that. She's just heard that she has pancreatic cancer and it's terminal."

"Oh, Dave," replied Gareth, "I'm sorry to hear that; that's really tough." He paused for a moment, looking thoughtful. "I guess I try to go through life not worrying too much about whether that might happen to me."

"I get that," said Dave, "but I do find myself asking the big questions a bit more these days. You know, about why we get old and die, what happens afterwards—those kinds of things."

Chapter 2

Getting Older

But if Christ is in you, although the body is dead because of sin, the Spirit is life because of righteousness.

Romans 8:10

I wonder if you've ever been part of a conversation at all like that. There's a lot of talk about the doctors "fixing" our bodies or our minds. Perhaps not so much about the bigger questions. So, with no apology, I want to write about getting older. "Oh, no," you say—especially if you are in your early fifties—"I am not ready for this! Must you?" Well, yes, I must. It's really important to think about it now, before "the evil days come and the years draw near of which you will say, 'I have no pleasure in them'" (Ecclesiastes 12:1).

What the apostle Paul writes in Romans 8:10 (above) encapsulates in a short space two very great truths if "Christ is in you". First, and negatively, that "the body is dead because of sin". Second, that "the Spirit is life because of righteousness". God the Holy Spirit is given to me in Christ, and he brings life even as I grow older. And therefore, as I walk through the afternoon of life, I live with this double thing happening in me. My body and mind grow older—and we will consider some of what this means in this chapter—and my spirit is being renewed by the Holy Spirit. I am one of those who "with unveiled face, beholding the glory of the Lord, are being transformed into the same image from one degree of glory to another" (2 Corinthians 3:18). So in this chapter we will also consider what it means to be inwardly renewed even as our bodies and minds decay.

Here, then, is what we need to do to be "Romans 8:10" believers as the years pass.

Come to Terms with "The Body Is Dead"

To say that "the body is dead" is an extraordinarily concise shorthand. The body means here all our existence in this world. It includes our physical bodies, with our bones, sinews, muscles, ligaments, joints, lungs, kidneys and so on. But it also encompasses our minds and indeed our embodied existence in all its dimensions. It means *me* as I am in this world—me in my entirety.

To say that "the body is dead" obviously cannot mean that it is literally dead, for it is clearly alive. My body moves, my heart beats, my blood flows, my mind thinks and so on. To say it is nevertheless "dead" is a shorthand way of saying that it is like a man condemned to death—"as good as dead", as it were, with every heartbeat shadowed by death. I am vulnerable to sickness and accident, to loss of memory, to mental illness. My body—*I*—lives in a bright world over which a dark cloud hangs, a cloud whose shadow touches everything about me.

The afternoon of life may be a time in which I become aware of this with a fresh intensity such that I begin to feel the cold fingers of death even in the simple processes of ageing. I want to encourage you, during this "in between" window of life, to come to terms with the undeniable fact that your body is under the sentence of death.

Now some of you will say, "Oh, this is much too gloomy. I feel I am in my prime. Why try to make me miserable like this?" Fair enough, perhaps you are. But, whether now or later, the time will come when you begin to feel yourself getting older.

Others may say, "All this is so obvious I can hardly believe you think it is worth saying. Besides, it's not a happy thought." Ah, but that's the point: it is not a happy thought. And, because it is not a happy thought, we don't want to think about it. We breathe the air of a culture that is in denial about death, not least because if we did think about it, the prospect would be too frightening, for the "fear of death" enslaves us (Hebrews 2:15).

But the disciple of Jesus has been set free from this slavery to fear and can face this fact head-on. It seems to me that there are different ways that we seek to deny or evade this. Many of us enjoy getting exercise or playing sport. Perhaps there is a sport at which we have excelled or simply one we have enjoyed for years. So we do our best to keep it up in the midst of the busyness of our lives. The level of team we play for begins to drop, from the first team to the second team and at some stage the veterans. Or we join a gym and work out regularly. Or we go jogging, swimming or hiking. All this is well and good. Our bodies are the temples of the Holy Spirit, and we ought to care for them. Indeed "bodily training is of some value" (1 Timothy 4:8).

The problem comes when this good stewardship of our bodies morphs into an idolatry of youth. When we resent the fact that our bodies are growing older, our energy levels are beginning to drop, our strength is decreasing, our stamina is compromised or our speed of reaction is slower. And so we step up the workouts in the gym. We do more and more exercise in a desperate attempt to slow the decline. We begin to care rather a lot for our stats on the running app. And we begin to show by our behaviour that we think that *bodily training is of very great value, almost supreme value.* I recognise this tendency in myself!

But we need to accept that the best efforts of a personal trainer or a physiotherapist can never bring more than temporary improvements to a dying body—a postponement of the inevitable end. They are, we might almost say, little better than palliative care. That may sound a little strong. And yet it is true. All our efforts to look after our bodies are little more than palliatives to make the (sometimes long-drawn-out) process of dying easier, and perhaps to stretch out our lives "by reason of strength", as Psalm 90:10 puts it.[3]

3 Alistair Begg sent me a cartoon in which a very stooped and decrepit old

The same question can surface in our attitudes to our appearance. We want to keep ourselves looking as good as we can. But we need to come to terms with the fact that the hair will go grey or fall out, the wrinkles cannot be held back for ever, the eyes will sometimes look tired. If looking good becomes an idol, then despair will follow close behind deterioration. But if I come to terms with my body being under the sentence of death, then, while I will look after myself as I can, I will accept the inevitable: I will gradually grow older.

A similar issue arises with our minds, and especially if we have been used to thinking with sharp logic or remembering with impressive recall or being freshly creative in our thoughts. All these things will decay, even if we never fall prey to some form of dementia (as many of us will). And that decay will begin to make itself known in our fifties, and most certainly in our sixties and seventies, even if it has been well masked in earlier years.

In all this, we accept that our energy levels are not what they were, that the time comes when we need a rest during the day, that we take longer to recover from travelling or some draining meeting, that we cannot expect to recall names, faces, or facts as once we did. We face this. We adjust our expectations and limit our chosen commitments so that we do not take on workloads that we could once sustain in our twenties or thirties. We learn to live with this. We are not constantly fighting against it. For we know that "the body is dead".

---

man sits before a physician, who says, "Remember the twenty extra years you added to your life through clean, healthy living? Well, these are them."

It is worth mentioning a mistake in the opposite direction. We turn fifty and think, "Oh no! It's all downhill from here". A pastor friend counsels me to warn of the danger of thinking you are older than you are. He mentions a man who keeps telling him that he is 57 and on the last stretch of his life. The pastor wants to say to him, "Stop thinking about yourself too much; just get on and live!" I agree. Do the next thing. Serve God today. By coming to terms with our mortality, I mean a quiet acquiescence, a humble sitting under the mighty hand of God, so that I am not constantly striving, as in the old stories of King Canute, to turn back the tide. Then you and I can walk this path with grace.

Accept That This Is "Because of Sin"

Paul writes, "The body is dead *because of sin*"—and I want now to focus on those words "because of sin". I need to come to terms not only with the fact that I walk in the shadow of death but with the root cause: that this is "because of sin". I get older because I am descended from Adam, who sinned—and because I, too, have inherited his sinful nature. As Paul put it, "Sin came into the world through one man, and death through sin" (Romans 5:12).

And so, the second step, once we have come to terms with the mortality of our bodies, is to make the link between ageing and sin. Not one in a hundred, even among Christians, does this. We think—and are coached by our Western cultures to think—in terms of physical causality for ageing. My knee hurts because of an old sporting injury, and that's all there is to it. We look at the physical causes of cancers or heart disease, and at the factors that may have caused psychological disorders, or whatever. But we need to look beyond the instrumental causes to the root cause. For to say that "the body is dead because of sin" is to acknowledge that "sin came into the world through one man, and death through sin, and so death spread to all men because all sinned" (v 12).

The word "death" means not only that moment when we breathe our last but a dark power that casts its shadow over all of life. Every sickness, from the most trivial to the most life-threatening, each accident, every decade of gradual ageing—all these are the shadow of death. Every one is the result of sin. It isn't necessarily, of course, that my individual and particular sin leads to this or that particular shadow of death; usually it does not although from time to time it may. But all of it comes to us because together we are sinners living in a world under God's righteous judgment.

It really goes against the grain to say, "My knee hurts because I am a sinner in a world under sin"; and yet it is true. I greatly used to enjoy playing tennis. But damage to my wrist has meant I have had to stop. Why did I have to give up? Because of damage to my wrist through too many serves and smashes? Yes, sure. But ultimately I had to give up tennis because of sin. It would be good if we began to weave this kind of talk into our Christian conversations.

Hate Sin in All Its Varying Forms

If indeed "the body is dead because of sin", then I will learn to transfer my feelings about mortality to my attitude towards sin. Nobody likes getting older. We all wish we did not grow weaker. No one wants to have an accident or welcomes being sick. Whenever age casts its shadow over our lives, we react with sorrow and dislike.

But we need to learn to let our hatred for our suffering move into a hatred for our sins. So here's the challenge: every time you dislike getting older or hate feeling ill, turn your aversion into a fresh hatred of your sin. Become a man or woman who hates sin more passionately with every passing year.

And watch for the besetting sins of each decade. For the sins of a sixty-something fill a different canvas from the iniquities of a forty-something. Be on the lookout for the newly stirred-up sins crowding into your life. You yourself may grow less vigorous; your sins do not. Even as your own energies decrease, your sins will attack you with unrelenting vigour. Temptations never get tired. They are like amateur actors, restlessly changing into new clothing with every passing scene of your life's drama.

In the Book of Common Prayer, there is a service for Ash Wednesday, the beginning of Lent. In one of the prayers, we ask God, "Mercifully forgive us our trespasses; receive and comfort us, who are *grieved and wearied with the burden of our sins*". We all know what it is to be grieved and wearied by the heavy burdens of our sufferings. We need to learn to be grieved and wearied with the burden of our sins. It is not only our ageing that feels heavy at times (as it does); we need to feel the burdensome weight of our sins. We feel this only when we really believe that the mortality of our bodies results from our sins. When we grasp this, even the most attractive of our sins begins to be seen in its true colours. Sin dresses up so that we want it. It promises us abundant life. But it is a fraud, for actually it can only give us death. So learn, with each passing year, to hate sin more.

Fight Sin in the Power of the Holy Spirit

From hating sin, it is a natural step to fighting sin. Romans 8 is full of this. There is a "law of sin and death" (v 2), from which God has set us free by the Spirit. The Spirit gives us grace to walk "not according to the flesh" (the old nature), "but according to the Spirit" (v 4). Every time I begin to feel my age, I am to say to myself, "This is because I am a sinner in a world under sin. How I hate my sins! Lord, give me grace today to hate sin more and to fight sin in my life." And so something dark (the shadow of death) stirs in me something bright (a fresh resolve to fight sin in my life). Renew the fight against sin. Take up your weapons of the Spirit to strive afresh against laziness, lust, greed, grumpiness, gossip, boasting, malice, untruths and whatever other sins beset and surround your heart.

If you have been a disciple for some years, you will know that the desires of your sinful nature wage war against the desires of the Holy Spirit within you. But to know this in your head is not the same as to be engaged actively in the battle. I can pretend I am still fighting sin when in reality I have raised the white flag some while ago.

So why not reread Galatians 5:16-26 and pray that these years will be characterised by an intentional walking by the Holy Spirit?

Sorrow with God's Groaning Creation

My fifth and sixth exhortations are less obvious entailments of ageing, but they arise from the broader context of Romans 8. Let me explain.

Romans 8 gloriously sets the mortal bodies of believers alongside the groaning and hope of the whole creation (v 19-22). The whole creation groans. It is "subjected to futility" (v 20), decaying in every part, infected with death, suffused with suffering. As a Western-culture person, I naturally think of myself as an individual. Ageing concerns *me*. It is I who am now in my fifties or sixties. Well, that is as may be. But it is not all about me (or about you). For I am not simply an individual; I am a part of a whole fallen humanity mis-governing the entire troubled creation.

It is right for us to feel the pain of our broken world perhaps more sharply as we get older. I am not speaking about that fanciful harking back to some imagined golden age, wishing we could rewind the clock, for it is foolishness to think like this (Ecclesiastes 7:10). But let us pray to develop a fresh sensitivity to the groaning of the whole created order under the sinful government of men and women. Let us sorrow for suffering men, women and children. Let us grieve when we have not stewarded the beauties of creation well. Let us lament to see something so good become so spoiled.

Marvel at God's Good Creation

But when we sorrow for the groaning creation, something else happens to us. For we remember that this good but spoiled creation will be made new; everything good in it will be purified so that it shines with a wonderful radiance in the new heavens and new earth. And therefore we begin to appreciate and enjoy with fresh eyes the wonder of God's creation—this magnificent theatre of the glory of God (as John Calvin called it).

Here is something perhaps surprising but heartening and hopeful for us. As we grow older, there is a sense in which the joys of this world begin to fade. We find we can no longer reach the peak of that mountain we once climbed; our pace is falling off from the running of our prime; our eyesight is not so keen to enjoy the wonders of a star through a telescope; and our hearing fails to savour the beauty of birdsong as it once did. And yet, even as our senses begin to decline, our heart's enjoyment of God's creation may be resensitised as never before. The simple joys of a May-morning picnic or a November walk by a river can thrill our hearts. For now we call to mind that all these things, which we once took for granted, are but the offscourings of the beauty of God and foretastes of the banquet of God's wonders in the new creation.

Many in their fifties and sixties learn to appreciate the created order with fresh eyes and ears of the heart.

A hobby such as working with wood, trying new foods, painting or sketching, learning a musical instrument, enjoying a movie or a concert—all these things may be signs of the Spirit of God being life in us. In these innocent delights, we may hope to see ourselves becoming men and women who show a lively interest in the world around us, and thereby to be interesting people, bubbling over with what we have found or seen or heard or discovered.

Hope for the Redemption of Our Bodies

Finally, a Romans-8 believer is shot through with hope. "The Spirit is life because of righteousness" (v 10). This compresses a great truth into a short space. God the Holy Spirit is given to me in Christ. He dwells within me. He brings with him the Father and the Son to make my heart their home (John 14:23).

He also brings the promise of eternal life. His presence guarantees resurrection. As I wait for the final redemption of my body (Romans 8:23), I know I will not wait in vain. And all this is "because of righteousness": not because of my merits—for I have no natural righteousness of my own—but the flawless righteousness of Jesus Christ given to me, reckoned to me, imputed to me by pure grace and gladly grasped with the empty hands of faith.

Thankfulness is therefore a great mark of the ageing believer. Every year that passes we feel—or ought to feel—more deeply our sinfulness, our frailty, the corruption of our nature. And yet with each passing month, we may find thanksgiving welling up and overflowing in our hearts for the forgiveness of our sins and for all the wonders of the gospel. On the one hand, I grow more limited and—or so it seems to me—more deeply sinful; on the other hand, I overflow in thankfulness for Jesus and all he is to me.

This may be a good moment to speak a word of hope as we lament the deterioration in our bodies. This is most beautifully expressed by the apostle Peter as he writes to Christian women as they grow older. He speaks of "the imperishable beauty of a gentle and quiet spirit, which in God's sight is very precious" (1 Peter 3:4). There is a huge worldwide beauty industry dedicated to making women feel (a) that they are not as beautiful as they would like to be and (b) that if they buy this product, they can become what they hope to be. But it is all an expensive way of fighting a losing battle. No matter how good the anti-wrinkle cream, the wrinkles will win in the end. But, says Peter, there is a beauty that is "imperishable". It needs no anti-wrinkle cream. It never perishes. In fact it grows more and more beautiful with age. This beauty is a loveliness of the heart—what Peter calls "a gentle and quiet spirit". And it is free. It needs no advertisements and charges no fee. Every woman in Christ can have this. And it just gets better and better! (If you'd like further to consider the particulars of ageing as a woman, my friend Sarah Allen has written an appendix on the menopause on page 173.)

One of the great motifs of Romans 8 is hope. We "wait eagerly for adoption as sons [that is, those with the privileges of inheritance], the redemption of our bodies" (v 23). And so, as we wait, we live in sure and certain hope. Perhaps the defining mark of a godly, ageing believer is hope. As we come to terms with ageing. As we accept that this is because of sins. As we learn to hate sin and to wage war against sin. As we groan with a spoiled creation and delight in the wonders of a still good creation, we know that our bodies will one day be redeemed, made new in glorious resurrection. We are descendants of Adam, and our bodies die in him. But there is a second Adam—Jesus Christ—and we belong to him. And so there is a brightness in the eyes of our hearts that can speak to a world in which hope is so hard to find. We never forget that "salvation is nearer to us now than when we first believed" (13:11).

Questions and Responses

1. In what ways are you becoming aware that you live under the shadow of death? What would a quiet acceptance of this look like for you?

2. "My knee hurts because I am a sinner in a world under sin." What would be an equivalent statement for you? How can you deepen your hatred of sin as you grow through these decades?"

3. In what ways are temptations changing for you at your stage of life? How can you fight these temptations as they shape-shift for you? In what ways is the battle of the flesh against the Spirit a matter of lively experience for you just now? Try to be specific.

4. Which miseries of life in a broken world are you feeling more keenly as you age? Are there ways in which you can learn to enjoy God's creation afresh at this stage of life? How can Romans 8 help you with this?

5. How can you ponder—and encourage others to ponder—the wonders of the hope that we have in Christ? Think of ways in which you can drip feed this hope into ordinary conversations.

Megan and Jeff, both in their early fifties, were chatting after church.

"You know," said Jeff, who was a teacher, "I've been thinking that after I retire I'd love to learn really to pray. I'm so busy at the moment that it's not possible. But later I hope I'll have time."

"Really?" said Megan, "I don't think you will. Other things will crowd in then, just as things squeeze out prayer now."

"What about you, then?" asked Jeff, knowing that Megan also had a high-pressure job as a senior accountant. "You're pretty busy at work, aren't you?"

"Well, yes, I am," said Megan. "But I've resolved to make prayer a priority in my life now and am trying to carve out more time for it. Ask me next Sunday how I'm getting on. That will help me to be accountable!"

Chapter 3

Prayer

Now there was a man in Jerusalem, whose name was Simeon, and this man was righteous and devout, waiting for the consolation of Israel, and the Holy Spirit was upon him.

And there was a prophetess, Anna … She did not depart from the temple, worshipping with fasting and prayer night and day.

Luke 2:25, 36-37

Megan is right, isn't she? In this chapter I want to encourage you to be a devoted warrior in prayer now, in the afternoon of life. And I want to do so by looking at two great intercessors in the evening of their lives. I want to set before you, as I set before myself, the shining examples of Simeon and Anna. I must admit that they are two of my favourite minor characters in the Bible. I want to give them Oscars for "best supporting actor and actress" in the Bible story! Both of them were in what I suppose we would call the evening of life; they were very old. But I want us to train ourselves in the "afternoon" so that we too may be great pray-ers in the "evening", if God grants us that.

Both Simeon and Anna understood that God had made wonderful covenant promises and granted believers the privilege of prayer, in which to claim those promises. The word "waiting" (for Simeon) is shorthand for all intercession (prayers on behalf of another). After all, that's what prayer is: a faith-filled waiting upon God as we call upon him to do what he has promised to do. The temple was their place of prayer, for they were believers under the old covenant, and they knew that God had promised that this should be the house of prayer, as Jesus would later say (Luke 19:46). We are told that Anna worshipped with fasting and prayer, and that she did so night and day. There seem to have been others with them "waiting for the redemption of Jerusalem" (Luke 2:38), no doubt holding prayer meetings in some part of the temple.

As new-covenant believers, we rejoice that we have access to God the Father through the name of God the Son and in the ministry of God the Holy Spirit (Ephesians 2:18). Simeon and Anna had this access too, although under the old covenant they may not have understood it so clearly. I want us to notice two features of their example.

Their Prayer Was Not in Vain

The first is this: their prayer was not in vain. They were waiting, watching, fasting and praying that God would send the Christ, the Messiah, to console and redeem his people. It seems they had been praying faithfully for a long time. And then one day, a young couple walked into the temple with their little boy and placed the boy in Simeon's arms, and immediately he knew that his wait had not been in vain (Luke 2:27-32). He and Anna and all who had waited and prayed with them now knew that God had kept his promise to send his Christ. What a day that was!

We now pray for the return of the Lord Jesus; we cry for the kingdom to come, for God's will to be done on earth as it is done in heaven (Matthew 6:10). All our prayers come under this umbrella. And, as we pray, we know that we are not engaged in empty wishful-thinking. We are claiming promises that God has made and every one of which he will keep. Prayer is always worth doing; it is guaranteed to succeed when we pray the promises of God. We do many things in life, and some may end in tears of disappointment. But never prayer, when it is according to the will of God.

We Can Go On Praying Into Old Age

The second feature is—or ought to be—very obvious: we can go on praying into old age. Where there is life there can be prayer. Our bodily muscles will in the end decay. But the muscles of prayer can grow firmer and stronger year after year after year. You and I can pray when we can no longer run or walk or even read or talk. So let us use our fifties and sixties to learn to pray, perhaps as never before, that we may be like Simeon and Anna if we live into old age.

Three Contexts for Our Prayers

So, if you are deeply convinced that prayer is never in vain and that you can hope to continue praying into old age, if God spares you, let me continue by discussing what we might call the three major contexts for prayer.

1. PRAY WITH YOUR CHURCH

The first—and really the normative—context is the corporate activity of the church at prayer. Before I pray—before even two or three of us pray—we all pray together as the church of Christ gathered in the presence of the Lord. So the first thing to say is this: make it a high priority during this window of life to join with your brothers and sisters in prayer in the church to which you belong.

I assume that your church prays together on a Sunday when you meet for worship. Prepare yourself for these special times. Ask God that your heart and soul may be entering fully into the prayers and praises of your church. As the minister, or another brother or sister, leads the congregation in prayer, say to yourself, "I, in the afternoon of my life, want to be eager and careful that I join my heart with my church family, so that my 'Amen' comes from my heart".

I imagine also that your church has meetings especially for prayer—perhaps a weekly or a monthly prayer meeting. Make these a priority. Be there if you possibly can be. Let it be that your minister will wake up on the morning of a prayer meeting and can say to himself, "I know that [*substitute your name*] will be there". If you cannot be there because of sickness or by reason of being away, let the minister know that you will be with your brothers and sisters in spirit and that you are sorry not to be there.

2. PRAY WITH ONE OR TWO OTHERS

The second context for prayer is praying with one or two others.

For those who are married, this will include praying regularly with your husband or wife if he or she is a believer. It took my wife and me many years of married life before we found a realistic pattern for prayer together. We started—as many Christian couples do—with unrealistic ambitions of grand seasons of prayer together. The reality, as we brought up our children in the busyness of our lives, was that our fine ambitions hung in the air as just that: ambitions and no more.

In more recent years, we have settled into a very ordinary pattern. After our (separate) morning devotions, we pray together for the day ahead—for those we expect to see or correspond with, for the tasks to be done, as well as for our family and others. We find it helpful each to have an old-fashioned paper planner devoted to prayer requests and needs. In it we write both needs for particular dates (so-and-so is helping with a Christian mission this week; someone else is getting married today; and so on) and other needs of which we have come to know. And then in the evening, one or both of us says a prayer: for our family again, for those we have seen or corresponded with during the day, for the tasks, encouragements and frustrations of the day, and so on. We do not generally pray for a very long time, either morning or evening. But we do pray together, almost without fail. Sometimes, when one of us is away, we manage to pray together over the phone. It has gradually come to be one of the bedrock disciplines of our married life.

For many of us, this second context will encompass regular prayer with a small group. For many years, I have found it a great blessing to pray roughly weekly with two other men. I miss it when I am away and cannot join with them. We learn to be honest with one another and to pray not simply for external needs but for our hearts, for our struggles against temptation and so on.

3. PRAY ON YOUR OWN

The third, and in some ways the most challenging context is individual prayer. Jesus teaches that unless our lives include times when we, as it were, close the door and pray simply to our heavenly Father, then our prayers with others so easily become hypocrisy—praying in order to be heard, seen and praised by people (Matthew 6:5-6). So be ambitious to develop healthy habits of individual and personal prayer.

I find this the hardest of all. I have learned to pray with my wife, with my prayer triplet, and with my church fellowship. But when I am away on my own, my weaknesses in personal prayer become painfully apparent. I can—so easily—simply forget to pray almost altogether.

I find it helpful to think of personal prayer as including (a) moment-by-moment personal dependence upon the Lord; (b) occasional or responsive prayer triggered by some meeting, some message or some particular need; and (c) regular prayer. Personal dependence does not come naturally to me, and perhaps I am not the only one, for personal dependence is the expression of faith, and faith is a supernatural work of God in us. Again and again, I need to remind myself, and to allow others to remind me, to pray when in need. It is embarrassing to admit this, but it is true. My wife has taught me so much about prayer that responds to the needs at hand. Again and again, when we receive some message or come back from meeting some person, she will say, "Why don't we pray for them *now*?" And she is right. And, when it comes to regular prayer, most of us need some plan or system to help us to remember those for whom we aim to pray regularly. Otherwise we simply won't remember.

Develop Your Prayer Life

So, after thinking about these three contexts—the corporate prayer of the church, prayer with a few others, and personal prayer—I want to encourage you to think about what we might call developing a rich palette of prayer. A young child may learn to paint with not much more than primary colours. A mature painter uses a broad, rich, nuanced palette of hues and tones. In a similar way, it is good for us to develop a growing palette of prayer.

The Psalms are perhaps God's greatest instrument to shape our prayers and our praises. If we forget to confess our sins, the Psalms teach us to do so. If we neglect to praise God simply for who he is, for the majesty and grandeur of his being, the Psalms put these words in our mouths. If we fail to lament, the Psalms show us how to do this in a godly way (as does the book of Lamentations). And so on. So I commend to you a regular diet of psalms—not just your favourite psalms but all the psalms. There are resources available to help us to speak and sing the Psalms as Christians.[4]

Speaking of singing—and speaking as one who has neglected this more than practised it—there is a rich place in our devotions for singing psalms and maybe some of the great old hymns. Just as we sing habitually in our churches, let us not be ashamed to sing with one or two others and to sing on our own.

To read a book about the theology and practice of prayer can help to bring fresh vigour and depth to our prayers. But don't let reading about prayer become a substitute for actually praying! Another practice some have found helpful is to keep some kind of journal or diary of prayer and then review it periodically and use it for thanksgiving.

One contribution that afternoon people can often make is to pray intentionally, regularly and faithfully for adult children, for sons-in-law and daughters-in-law, for grandchildren, for godchildren and for wider

---

4 For an accessible introduction to the Psalms, you could try *Psalms For You* (The Good Book Company, 2020). For a more in-depth study, I have also written a four-volume commentary called *The Psalms: A Christ-Centered Commentary* (Crossway, 2024). As well as traditional metrical psalms (e.g. *Sing Psalms* from the Free Church of Scotland), there are lots of artists who have set psalms to contemporary music; you may want to start by exploring the work of Matt Searles (*Psalms for Congregations*) or Shane & Shane (*Psalms*).

family. Every believer ought to do this, of course, but these decades may be a particular opportunity to be intentional about this. Included in this will be regular, unflagging prayer for prodigals—for those members of our families who have turned away from the Saviour who loves them. It is not easy to pray day after day, week after week, month after month for such prodigals, especially when they seem pretty happily settled in the far country. It was not for nothing that Jesus taught the parable of the persistent widow so that we might pray and not lose heart in our prayers (Luke 18:1-8).

It is good to be reminded, when praying for family, to give priority to the deepest needs. Always we pray for that supernatural work of God's Spirit in their hearts. If they are not as yet believers, we cry to God that he will give them new birth by his Spirit. If they are believers, we yearn that Christ's Spirit will grow his fruit in them, will guard them from falling into temptation and will make them more like Jesus, as the Scriptures promise he will. Of course, we pray for their health, their day-to-day needs and all the normal stuff of life. But these things have a way of muscling into the foreground of our intercessions and of squeezing the gracious working of the Holy Spirit into a back corner. This we must resist.

Another opportunity to enrich the palette of our prayers is to pray more seriously for mission partners. Many send out prayer letters. Perhaps this is a time not only to subscribe to some more of these but actually to read them, to reply encouragingly to them, and most of all to pray for those who send them. This takes time and effort. It will never be wasted time. Something similar applies to newsletters, such as are often produced in churches or by mission agencies. It is good for every believer to use these. But the "not old, not young" stage of life may be a time to embrace this with a fresh, glad enthusiasm.

Two Obstacles to Prayer

1. IT IS EASIER "TOMORROW"

Let me close this chapter by mentioning two obstacles. The first is procrastination. It is very easy to read a chapter like this and say to yourself, "Well, this sounds a good idea. I will store this up, and later on, when I have a bit more time, I'll think about what I might do about it." That's what Jeff said at the start of the chapter. We all do this. Certainly I do. But it is better to do something modest today, however weak and inadequate, than to think vaguely about doing great things tomorrow. Resolve today to devote yourself to prayer and take some definite step, even if it is a very ordinary one. And then, as God brings you through this "afternoon" window of life, you will find yourself growing in joyful prayer.

2. IT IS HARD WORK

The second obstacle is simply this: prayer is hard work. Oh, sure, it is joyful; it is the highest calling of a man or woman in the image of God; it is the best and greatest thing we can do. But for sinful men and women to pray involves a wrestling (Colossians 4:12). We will never do this naturally. The old me cries out against it. So don't be surprised when it feels hard. That is just how it is. Don't let hard work put you off.

So, back to my heroes Simeon and Anna: would you not love to be like them? I would. Ponder then the blessings of learning a life of prayer in these decades of life. Resolve to grow as a believer who truly prays. And rejoice at such a great privilege.

Questions and Responses

1. Do you want to pray? Be honest. Reflect again on Simeon and Anna, and let their example stir you to want to pray.

2. How can you devote yourself more gladly to prayer with your church?

3. Do you pray with one or two others regularly? Could this be a good time to begin this practice?

4. Are there practical ways in which you can develop more faithful habits of personal prayer? Choose one of the suggestions above (under the heading "Develop Your Prayer Life") and be intentional about doing it.

It was New Year's Eve. Jenny and Lisa were chatting about their hopes for the coming year. Jenny's eyes lit up as she described her plans for a special holiday to celebrate her 60th birthday. She enthused over the comfort of a newly acquired car. She was a joyful evangelist for great vacations and terrific automobiles.

"What about you?" she asked Lisa, having finally run out of steam.

Lisa thought for a moment and said, "Well, I've got several nice things planned with friends. But for me, the thing I'm most excited about is that I'm going on a short-term mission trip"—and she mentioned a country in eastern Europe. "I'm going with a group to help with an outreach in their city and support a new church plant. I'm really looking forward to that."

Chapter 4

The Gospel

Whoever loses his life for my sake and the gospel's will save it.

Mark 8:35

Do not be ashamed of the testimony about our Lord, nor of me his prisoner, but share in suffering for the gospel by the power of God, who saved us and called us to a holy calling, not because of our works but because of his own purpose and grace, which he gave us in Christ Jesus before the ages began, and which now has been manifested through the appearing of our Saviour Christ Jesus, who abolished death and brought life and immortality to light through the gospel.

2 Timothy 1:8-10

In this chapter I want to encourage you to be gripped afresh by the life-changing gospel. I wonder if you have ever spoken like Jenny or like Lisa. I suspect most of us have echoed each of them at different times. I know there have been many occasions on which I have spoken like Jenny and rather wish I had spoken more like Lisa. How about you?

The challenge to take up the cross day by day (Luke 9:23) must be heard at every stage of life. There are reasons why it needs to be heard afresh in our fifties and sixties for, as we shall see, there are reasons why we may be tempted to draw back from such wholehearted discipleship. Before we think about what it may mean to be zealous for the gospel, I want to set before you a vision and motivation so that you long to be like this.

The Vision and Promise of the Gospel

When challenging disciples to take up the cross, Jesus adds this remarkable promise: that even as the person who wants to save his life will lose it, so whoever loses his life for Jesus and his gospel will save it. When I am tempted to back-pedal on my zeal and to guard and cosset my life (after all, I think to myself, I am beginning to grow a little older and more tired, and besides which I surely deserve a break, don't I?), I need to remember Jesus' promise: if day by day I give myself in costly service for Jesus and his gospel, then I will save my life. The challenge therefore to be gospel-wholehearted in the afternoon of life is not simply a "blood, sweat, toil and tears" appeal; it is the offer of the only life that lasts and the single hope for my life and soul.

When writing to Timothy in Ephesus (2 Timothy 1:8-10 above), Paul calls him to share in suffering for the gospel—but then he pours out a wildly exuberant vision of the gospel, in which death itself is abolished and life and immortality are brought to light. Many of us, as we reach our fifties and beyond, need this reminder. Perhaps, if we were believers in our teens or twenties, we responded with joy to the challenge of a life given sacrificially for the gospel. Perhaps we sang, "Take my life, and let it be, consecrated, Lord, to thee" with a glad zeal. Maybe we followed this up in some costly service of Christ's gospel. Let us hear this again in our fifties and sixties, for the promises are as true for us now as they were then. The gospel is as wonderful now as it was then. Indeed, as our own deaths grow a little closer, the gospel is more precious than ever and Jesus more worthy of our service.

So what might it mean for you to be gripped by a zeal for Christ and his gospel that burns brightly through your fifties, brighter still during your sixties, and yet more radiantly in your seventies? What might this look like in practice? It will be different for each of us, of course. But here are some ideas, beginning with the most visibly radical. Each is powered by passion for Jesus.

A Completely New Adventure for the Gospel

I suppose that, for many of us, our fifties and sixties are a time of steadiness and settled activity. Perhaps you have been engaged in an occupation for one or two decades or more. Your general expectation is that you will carry on with that same occupation, perhaps slowing down a little as you move towards retirement, or maybe enjoying a long-awaited promotion and embracing bigger responsibilities, but all driving along the same general activity pathway. There is nothing necessarily wrong with this. But let me throw a stone into these calm waters. How about doing something completely different? What about bringing your present occupation to a close, perhaps a decade or more earlier than you had anticipated? And then embarking on some very different adventure with God to serve the gospel of Jesus?

Why not say to yourself something like this: "I yearn for my life to count for Jesus. I would be so sad to see my life just dribble away in drops of predictable lifestyle. Or, worse still, to feel myself squeezed into the mould of a world without God. I do not know how many more years the Lord will give me. But I want every one of them to count for Jesus as only he knows how. And so, rather than drifting towards retirement, I resolve to be actively intentional, seeking some way to serve the gospel in this window of my life."

I remember a colleague telling me that he and his wife, each aged about 60 (as I remember), had decided to move from the UK to sub-saharan Africa to work in cross-cultural mission. "I think I have one more spell of active service in me," he said, "and my wife and I want to use it for Jesus". And so they did. They packed up and moved to Africa to serve churches there, using their gifts and experience in the afternoon of their lives. I remember being very struck by just how radical, and yet how eminently reasonable, this was. Neither this man nor his wife were the sort of characters you would call wild adventurers. There are people for whom we are not in the least surprised when they do something unpredictable; but these were not they. They were sensible, sober, cool-headed people. And in their sensible, sober, cool-headed way they did something that dramatically challenged the usual expectations, not only of their non-Christian friends but of most of their Christian brothers and sisters. It was a simple but, to me, memorable action.

Might you be able to do something like this? It is not unusual for mission agencies and churches in other countries to seek men and women in the afternoon of life. Such men and women cannot offer the boundless energy of folks in their twenties and thirties. Perhaps it is too late for the rigours of learning a new and difficult language. But they often have a maturity bred from experience over the years—both a simple human maturity and a spiritual maturity. They have seen the gospel at work over decades. They know in experience that this is how God saves. And they can contribute something that the much younger cross-cultural mission partners cannot. Perhaps this might be you.

Of course, there may be God-given reasons why you cannot do this: reasons perhaps of caring for elderly parents (see chapter 5) or for sons or daughters with ongoing special needs. But let me encourage you not to write off this idea too easily.

Or how about moving to a different part of your own country to support a church plant or a church with few resources? Perhaps you have grown quite comfortable in your own church. You have long friendships there. You are accustomed to the ways things are done. It feels somehow homely and predictable. The thought of relocating to an area you may not know (or even like), to throw your weight behind a church that is new or struggling, is unsettling to say the least. But how about it?

Some of these radical ideas may involve taking early retirement if this is offered to you. There may be implications for your pension, and you do not want to act without carefully counting the cost. Sure, but Jesus speaks about taking up the cross and losing your life. Do not dismiss these radical ideas out of hand.

There may be ways in which you can do some training for Christian ministry in this window of life—some study or some mix of study and practical experience. When I was working at the Cornhill Training Course in London, we not infrequently had some men and women in their fifties and sixties working hard to train like this. Most students were in their twenties or thirties, as we might expect. But those in the afternoon of life contributed something distinctive to the course. We were so glad to have them, and we could see how God was already using them for the gospel of Jesus.

Your Money for the Gospel

Jesus taught often about money, both its dangers and its opportunities. The afternoon of life is perhaps a time when both are heightened. If you are one who is enjoying more money than before, think about how you will use it. Perhaps you have had promotions that mean you are earning well. Maybe you have inherited funds from parents. It could be that your children have left home and are making their own way through life without being financially dependent upon you. One way or another, you find you have capital that perhaps you never dreamed of before. Or you are finding that your regular income is more than sufficient for your needs. Of course, there are plenty of people for whom this paints a picture of a dreamworld; their realities are very different. But just suppose that, in some measure, this is you. What then?

There are, broadly speaking, two pathways you can tread. Down one street—well-populated by afternoon men and women—walk those who are gradually improving their standard of living. The cars get faster or more comfortable. We watch them upsize or remodel to a more desirable home. The holidays move up to a higher level, the gizmos are better models and bought more quickly, the furniture and curtains are just that bit more fashionable and so on. There may be nothing wrong with this. Some of these things may indeed be wise as we grow a little older and need a bit more help in life. But the whole "steadily improving standard of living" slope is fraught with danger. It is so easy to lose our first love for Jesus, to blunt our zeal for the gospel, to live as if this world could be our home.

So take a look at the other fork: a narrow road that is hard to walk because it is steep and overhung by brambles and nettles. On this path are afternoon men and women resolved to use their new-found money for the gospel of Jesus. It is not easy. But with great joy, they invest far larger sums of money—both capital and income—into gospel people and gospel projects. They find themselves giving sums they could never have dreamed of passing on. And in so doing, they find an exhilaration—a sense of wonder that to them of all people is given this grace of giving (2 Corinthians 8:7).

Let me ask you. Would you not rather be on this second road? Does not your heart sing at the thought of glad generosity? Are you not filled with wonder at the thought that you might be entrusted with riches in order to use them for the gospel of Jesus? It may be that your circumstances prevent you from embarking on the wild adventures such as I described above. And yet God places money in your bank accounts and portfolios that you may share in these adventures for the gospel. What a joy to be gospel partners![5]

All My Days for the Gospel

My third focus is our time. As with every suggestion here, you may read what follows and say that you could only wish this was true for you. But some will read this and recognise themselves. If so, read on.

Just suppose, then, that your children have left—or, if young adults, partly left—home. The relentless pressures of child-rearing are over. Suppose that your parents are not in need of heavy care. That your job is manageable. All in all, that you have more time at your disposal. Of course, we all know what it is to have hordes of time invaders—

5 Many have been inspired by the stories in the book *Gospel Patrons* by John Rinehart (Gospel Patrons, 2014).

those often petty tasks or distractions that creep across the borders of your calendar day by day and invade those dreamed-of open spaces of free time. But, even allowing for these, you do have more choice now about how you spend at least part of your weeks. What then?

As with money, I suppose there can be a fork in the road. In one direction there is a happy throng of those who fill these spaces with enjoyable activities. They take more vacations—perhaps many more. Always they seem to be planning a new trip, travelling to a fresh location, relaxing in an exotic place, or recounting stories about it on their return, just in time to begin planning the next cruise or flight. Their sporting time grows, even as their sporting prowess diminishes and the choice of sports reflects their age (from rugby to golf and finally carpet bowls!). They embrace a new hobby with enthusiasm. And—and here's the thing—they do all this in such a way that every nook and cranny in their newly freed-up calendar is filled. The things they do are—or may be—good, wholesome, creative and life-enhancing. But it is an open question whether filling every time slot really serves the gospel.

So let's take a look at the other direction from this fork. On this path are men and women who certainly take trips, enjoy sports, embrace hobbies and generally thrive on the good gifts God gives. They are not kill-joys. Far from it. But—and here is the difference—they have asked themselves first if there is some gospel service that can be given a high priority in their new-found time. They have perhaps an adequate salary or pension. They do not need to be paid for their service. But they look for openings to volunteer in ways that serve the gospel of Jesus. Every church has such needs. Most churches are blessed by the glad giving of time from men and women in the afternoon of life. It may be helping with something administrative or assisting with a lunch club for the elderly or being on the rota for a toddler group or contributing to some catering need or filling a gap in practical care for a building or garden. The men and women on this road look at the recently opened-up windows of time in their calendars. And the first question they ask is "In the midst of a time-starved culture, how can I use this precious gift to serve the gospel of Jesus?"

Every Friendship for the Gospel

The final area to consider is the sharing of the gospel. This will include what we sometimes call personal evangelism, when a believer shares the gospel with an unbeliever. Some afternoon people intentionally cultivate friendships with unbelievers and use their time and money to move beyond the superficiality of so many modern relationships. They actively invest in these friendships even though they are not as comfortable as spending time with Christian brothers and sisters. They pray for openings to speak of Jesus. They let these unbelievers watch their lives, they listen carefully in conversation, and they look through windows of friendship into the other person's heart so that they may begin to sense what makes them tick. And then, as and when God opens ears, they take every opportunity to speak of the gospel of Jesus.

Some Christians are conspicuously gifted at personal evangelism. Others of us—and I include myself—are not. This does not excuse us from praying for opportunities and asking for courage and grace to take them when God gives them. But it is encouraging for us to remember that there are other ways in which we may use our friendships for the gospel. Prominent among these is that we may draw friends into a friendship group in which Christians who are gifted at sharing the gospel can meet them. We may be, as it were, catalysts for evangelism, as well as seeking to do evangelism ourselves. But, however we do this, our hearts will be set with longing that those without Christ will come under the sound of the gospel and be drawn into the life-giving light of Christ.

How will you be gripped afresh by the gospel in these decades? For you it may be one or all of the things we've considered: a grand and radical new adventure, a fresh resolution with your money, a gospel focus for your time, and the intentional use of friendships for Christ. However you do it, as you live through your fifties and sixties, keep these words of Jesus ringing in your ears: "Whoever loses his life for my sake and the gospel's will save it" (Mark 8:35).

Questions and Responses

1. Does the gospel thrill you as perhaps once it did? Be honest. If it doesn't, don't jump to the practical ideas in this chapter. Take time to ponder the riches and wonder of the gospel of Christ until your heart again sings with joy.

2. Consider seriously the idea of a radical adventure for the gospel at this stage of life. Might this be possible for you?

3. Review your money and how you spend it. Could it be that the Lord is opening a window of opportunity to give more joyfully and generously for the gospel?

4. And how about your time? Review your schedule and consider your priorities. Don't beat yourself over the head with guilt, but ask yourself if there is a more joyfully gospel-focused use of your time that might be your choice today?

5. Consider how your life and friendships can contribute to the sharing of the good news of Jesus. Are there changes you can cheerfully make?

Mike and Ellie have three teenage children. The oldest is just off to college this autumn. Mike's dad died ten years ago and his mother lives nearby enjoying good health in her early eighties. Ellie's mum has just died suddenly and unexpectedly. Her dad is quite frail, in his mid-eighties, and lives a five-hour drive away. Ellie is an only child. Her mother's death has raised urgent questions about her dad's care in his old age.

Chapter 5

Elderly Parents

Honour your father and mother, that your days may be long in the land that the LORD your God is giving you.

Exodus 20:12

But if a widow has children or grandchildren, let them first learn to show godliness to their own household and to make some return to their parents, for this is pleasing in the sight of God.

1 Timothy 5:4

This chapter speaks to those who are grappling with questions like the ones faced by Ellie and Mike. With life expectancy at unprecedentedly high levels in some prosperous western nations, the "afternooners" are sometimes described as "the sandwich generation", with elderly parents on one side and children on the other, sandwiched in the middle and sometimes pulled in both directions at once. This chapter focuses on the top layer of the sandwich (the elderly parents), while chapter 7 speaks about the lower level (the younger generations of our families).

There Are Parents and Parents

Elderly parents come in all shapes and sizes (if I may put it like this). Some are believers, and others are not. Some are married and in good health. Many are on the other side of broken marriages, perhaps with a new partner. Some live close to one or more of their children; others do not. Some have good and wholesome relations with their family, but others live with the scars of a dark, sad history of relational breakdown.

Some have sufficient money with which to live quite comfortably, perhaps in their own home. The home itself may be the house in which they raised their children; perhaps they have downsized, or maybe they haven't. Some are in pretty decent health for their age and can still live independently, do their own shopping and cooking, keep up friendships and be an active presence in their church or community. Many are more frail, with failing health, which may include both physical weakness and mental decay.

In most families there is a double movement that begins with mothers and fathers caring 100% for a newborn baby and ends with the grown-up son or daughter caring close to 100% for the aged parent. I remember a friend of mine reflecting on this as he fed his frail mother with a spoon in her hospital bed. The reversal of roles can be intensely striking. And it usually happens gradually. As a younger adult, we attain a healthy independence, but—often for many years—the mother or father continues to be a net contributor to the family ecosystem, giving time, energy and money, being a welcome help rather than a drain and a hindrance. But gradually this changes as the mother or father becomes increasingly dependent upon a son or daughter for their needs.

Questions faced by "afternooners" with elderly parents are legion. They may include:

- What are their current needs—physically, mentally, spiritually and emotionally?
- How often should I visit, and how can I make my visits good times for them?
- Can we, or should we, have him/her/them come to live with us or near us?
- If so, when would be the right time to uproot them from their home and networks of friendships and perhaps church?
- Ought I to uproot myself and go and live with them, or near them, so that I can care for them?
- Above all, how best can I love and honour them?

This book cannot answer these questions for you. But I hope it can help you take a step back and consider the principles, and the wisdom, given us by God in the Bible. So let's do that now.

The Great Commandment

Before we come to the fifth commandment, let us take a step even further back and think about what Jesus calls "the great commandment". When asked about this, Jesus gives an answer that deserves rather careful thought. First, he quotes from the *Shema* in Deuteronomy 6:5 with the words, "You shall love the Lord your God with all your heart and with all your soul and with all your mind" and says, "This is the great and first commandment". But then he continues, "And a second is like it: You shall love your neighbour as yourself" (quoting Leviticus 19:18). "On these two commandments depend all the Law and the Prophets" (Matthew 22:37-40). But how are these two commandments related?

It is easy to think that we have to do some kind of balancing act: to make sure we love God lots but not at the expense of loving our neighbours, and that we love our neighbours a fair bit but not so that we forget to love God. It would be hard to think of a more disastrous misunderstanding. This places a cruel burden on us, since we necessarily fail with both. And it is just plain wrong. We are to love God with all that we are—all our heart, soul, mind and strength. Not just some of it; all of it. We love our neighbours not as an alternative to loving God but precisely *because* we love God, and it is God who places a neighbour close to us.

But which neighbour? Who is my neighbour (to echo the lawyer's question in Luke 10:29)? Some answers are very clear in the Bible. One is that my mother and father are placed before me by God that I may honour them.

I may or may not be fond of them. I may or may not find it easy. But, if I love God, then I will demonstrate this by loving my mother and father. God will place other neighbours in front of us to love: some for many years (a husband, wife, or child) and some for shorter periods of time (a colleague, a friend, the folks on our street). But, so long as I live and so long as my mum and dad live, God says to me, *Honour them!*

The fifth commandment comes in this context. It is, as Paul notes, the first commandment with a promise: "that your days may be long in the land" (Ephesians 6:2). Under the old covenant this is the promised land. But why does honouring parents make for a long stay in the land? There is a long tradition of understanding the fifth commandment to be the tip of a moral iceberg consisting of our obligations to honour those set in authority over us. A society that honours mother and father will be one in which the proper ordering of society will make for stability and thus longevity.

Sons and daughters, when children, are to obey their parents (e.g. Ephesians 6:1); adult sons and daughters are not bound by this command. But we are still to honour our parents. What does this mean? It means to treat them as significant, as people who matter, and to do that simply because they are our mother and father. This honour is not dependent on how good the parents may or may not have been; it is because they are mother and father. A healthy society is one in which sons and daughters treat their parents as people who matter, people to be loved and cared for, right into their old age.

Many Western societies resent this and prefer that aging parents are shut away when they become a drain on our time and money. Christians are to be shiningly counter-cultural in this.

In his public ministry, Jesus rebuked those who used religion as an excuse to avoid caring for their parents (Mark 7:9-13). Paul followed in his master's footsteps when he wrote to Timothy about the church's care for widows. Although the church has a responsibility to care for genuine godly widows, there is an exception: "But if a widow has children or grandchildren, let them first learn to show godliness to their own household and to make some return to their parents, for this is pleasing in the sight of God" (1 Timothy 5:4). The expression "to make some return" is very suggestive of the shift in care from that of parent for child to that of son or daughter for parent. Our parents did for us all manner of things, most of which we do not remember at all. But it was costly for them in time, in sleep deprivation, in love, in care and in money. Now it is time "to make some return".

So it is not difficult for Christian believers to be sure that they ought to honour and care for elderly parents. I remember a friend of mine explaining to her minister why she needed to leave her ministry position on his staff in order to go and care for her parents, as she is still doing. Much as he hated to lose her—for she was a superb Christian worker—he had to admit to her that he could hardly counsel her to break the fifth commandment!

How to Obey the Fifth Commandment

But what will this mean in practice?

1. MAKE IT A PRIORITY

First, it means that care for our elderly parents will be a high priority. We will have other obligations, perhaps especially to our wife or husband or our own children, and responsibilities in our churches and to our neighbours and friends. These also are the neighbours whom God places before us and calls us to love. But parents are going to be high on the list, in the light of the fifth commandment.

2. OPPOSE TALK OF ASSISTED SUICIDE

Second, Christian believers will distance themselves from all talk of the elderly being an unwanted burden. With assisted suicide now legalised in several nations, it is all too easy for such a terrible attitude quietly to infiltrate our thinking. Or perhaps we may find ourselves in a situation where our parent begins to wonder out loud whether it would be better for everyone if they pursued that option. After all, the longer they live, the more of our hoped-for inheritance is being used for their care and the more of our time is "drained" in looking after them.

Although the main motivation for assisted suicide is the alleviation of suffering—both of the sick person themselves and those who watch them suffer—this proposed remedy devalues human life in the image of God. Christian people will therefore shudder with horror at the idea of assisted suicide, and we will be vocal in our affirmation of the dignity of life and the beauty of dependence.

3. CARE FOR THEIR SPIRITUAL WELFARE

The spiritual welfare of elderly parents is easily neglected but absolutely vital. If they are not as yet believers, pray earnestly that God will have mercy on them. If they are believers, ask God to keep his promise to uphold them firmly to the end. Take opportunities to read the Bible and pray with them, and perhaps to sing hymns, psalms or songs with them. They may not be willing for you to do this, in which case you should respect their wishes, but do not be too shy about asking again; many will change their minds and even their hearts by the mercy of God. If they are willing for you to do this, do not neglect this privilege and honour.

4. COUNT THE COST

We do well to remember that this high calling is usually unexciting, unromantic and unimpressive. Most of it will be hidden from the eyes of the watching world. Much of it will be humdrum. Some of it will be physically unpleasant or emotionally distressing. It is good to recognise this. It may involve cancelling a holiday or passing on career advancement. Caring for my parents in their closing years was one factor that led me to a nervous breakdown. But it is a calling from God and therefore something that God will honour.

My parents were sweet and kind. But we must face the fact that some parents can be obnoxious. (As I write this, I pray that I will not be one such.) They can be quarrelsome, ungrateful, persistent grumblers. It can be really hard to honour them. If your parents are like this, pray to be set free from resentment and bitterness, which can so easily become a cancer eating into your soul. If you have parents who are shining examples of contentment and thankfulness, be very grateful, and pray for your friends who experience the opposite.

5. RECOGNISE THAT RESPONSIBILITIES CHANGE OVER TIME

Fifth, be ready to change. At one stage of life, there may be virtually no need to do more than make regular happy visits and phone calls. At another stage of life, we may need to drop almost everything to deal with crises. And much in between. Those of us—like me—who prefer life to be predictable need to be prepared for obedience to God in days of unpredictability. The medical crises are not amenable to prior entry in our calendars.

Even as steady and loyal sons and daughters, we can get used to one stage of our parents' lives and fail to recognise when their health or circumstances have changed. Perhaps what was once sufficient to honour them now needs to be raised to a new level.

6. EXPECT UNEXPECTED JOYS

There can be a strange joy in time spent with elderly parents as we perhaps reconnect with them after years of unintended distance and busyness (theirs as well as ours). To sit with your mother or father, to listen to them, to chat with them, to make them a cup of tea, to weep with them, to share some of the joys of life with them, to bring grandchildren to visit them—these can be precious days. Memories can be made in old age just as they can be formed in childhood.

7. SEEK WISDOM

We will need wisdom from God to know how, what, when and where to help. Those of us who are married need to be prepared to spend time talking, listening and praying with our husband or wife about this. We care together for all our parents. But it is very natural to feel one way about our own parents and differently about our parents-in-law. Let's make sure that as married couples we really own the way we care for both sets of parents.

8. DO NOT BE GUILTY ABOUT WHAT YOU CANNOT DO

It's easy to be consumed with guilt when we long to help but cannot. I watch a nurse friend moving house to care for her elderly mother—medically, physically and emotionally—and I say to myself, "I wish I could have done that for my parents". But I could not. It is wrong to place a parent in a nursing home as an easy way out of honouring them, to get them out of the way. But it is not always wrong to place them in a home because we are physically or medically unable to care for them as they need. It is simply beyond us, much as we might wish to do it. If that day comes, then we can honour them by frequent visits, by sitting with them, by doing all we can to ensure that the care in the home is kind and capable. It is a beautiful thing when the staff of a care home notice this. In the closing months of my own mother's life, I remember one of the staff saying to my wife, "You are like a daughter to her", as indeed she was in the kindness and fondness of her love. Her love reminded me of Ruth's for Naomi in the book of Ruth, and that was a beautiful thing.

9. PREPARE WELL FOR YOUR OWN OLD AGE

Finally, when we care for our own elderly parents, this can and should be a timely reminder to us to prepare well for our own old age, if God spares us. As we watch our parents, we cannot avoid noticing good and not so good aspects of how they may have prepared. There are several ways we can prepare, all of which ought to be obvious but sadly are often not. One is to be willing to downsize our home, in good time if we can, so that we do the lion's share of the sorting out and passing on of our possessions rather than leaving our long-suffering children to do this after we die or are no longer able. Another is to keep our wills up to date and to make provision for Powers of Attorney so that our children have the authority to manage our financial affairs and to make decisions about our health when we are no longer capable of this. A third is to keep short accounts in our family relationships, doing all in our power to live at peace even with the most difficult members of our families (see Romans 12:18).

It is also prudent to look for an opportunity to move to live close to one of our children before it is too late. This is often easier said than done, and it cannot reasonably be done until at least one of our children is well settled in a location (otherwise we risk becoming rather tiresome camp followers!). And we will not do this too soon, for it involves uprooting ourselves from our church, our neighbourhoods, and all our support networks of friends. Indeed, to do this too soon risks simply adding to the strain on our families as they have to try to replace as much as they can of the life we have previously led. It takes wisdom to do this at the right time, and sometimes this may not be in our control. But it is worth trying to do this and watching for an appropriate opportunity.

Honouring parents isn't easy. It may or may not be appreciated by them. But our Father in heaven sees and knows. In honouring them we are honouring him. And his reward is great.

Questions and Responses

1. List out the main "ingredients" of your current situation so far as elderly parents are concerned. Think about ages, marriages, health, location, mental health and finances.

2. In what current ways can or ought you to care for elderly parents, if you or your husband/wife have them? What are the immediate needs, if any?

3. What needs are to be expected in the next three or four years? How can you make preparations for these?

4. Are there longer-term preparations you could—and perhaps should—make?

5. What practical steps can I take to make it easier for my family to care for me if I live into frail old age?

6. Above all, pray earnestly that God will give you grace to respond gladly and willingly to the call of the fifth commandment.

Ben and Gary were chatting at a barbecue. They had become good friends in their early fifties. Ben confided in Gary that marriage wasn't easy. He hinted that there wasn't a lot of good sex. He spoke of frequent quarrels. He said that he and his wife seemed often to be pulling in different directions. Gary's wife had died in her forties, and Gary hadn't married again (at least not yet).

To Ben's surprise, Gary encouraged Ben to pray specifically about sex, to be super careful about temptation, and to let the gospel of Jesus pour its joyful nourishment into his troubled marriage. He prayed for Ben and his wife to enjoy a renewed friendship and that this would be like fuel for all the dimensions of their marriage. Ben was astonished to hear these generous-hearted and wise words from his widowed friend, who had lost all these blessings.

Chapter 6

Marriage

What therefore God has joined together, let not man separate.

Matthew 19:6

"Therefore a man shall leave his father and mother and hold fast to his wife, and the two shall become one flesh." This mystery is profound, and I am saying that it refers to Christ and the church.

Ephesians 5:31-32

Let marriage be held in honour among all, and let the marriage bed be undefiled, for God will judge the sexually immoral and adulterous.

Hebrews 13:4

In this chapter, I do not want to speak only to those of us who are married; I also want to write for those who are bereaved or divorced, or have never married. The words

"Let marriage be held in honour among all" sum it up.

My motivation is that astonishing statement in Ephesians 5:32 (above): that marriage "refers to Christ and the church". This picks up a tremendous Old Testament theme: that God is the bridegroom or husband of his covenant people, who are his bride. In the New Testament, Jesus speaks of himself as the bridegroom (Mark 2:19-20), who prepares his bride, his church, to be spotless on her wedding day (Revelation 19:7-8). That day will be one of overwhelming joy, delight and satisfaction. It is worth waiting for! And the marriages of men and women in this age—albeit mostly very ordinary and often quite difficult—are signs of this ultimate marriage. For this reason, it is both right and wonderfully necessary that we hold marriage in honour.

To Those Who Are Not Married

Let me begin with those who are walking through their fifties and sixties unmarried.

It may be that you have been widowed early and have tasted the bitter sadness of this loss. Or perhaps you are on the other side of the miseries of divorce, be that completely uncaused by you or with memories of what you yourself have said or done wrong. Or you may never have been married. Whatever your situation, the fifties and sixties can be a time when thoughts turn to what might have been. "If only" can come to haunt our daydreams.

And yet, for you in your unmarried state, it is nonetheless a privilege—albeit often a costly privilege—to keep marriage in honour. What you can do to make marriage a clear and shining picture of the marriage of Christ and his church is perhaps no less significant than what married men and women can do to this end. Let's consider what that involves.

1. LOOK FORWARD TO YOUR WEDDING DAY!

To you, whoever you are, I want to say this: never forget that God has your wedding day in his diary. That day will be a season of the most overwhelming joy and delight. If you belong to Jesus, then these words are yours: "Let us rejoice and exult and give him the glory, for the marriage of the Lamb has come, and his Bride has made herself ready; it was granted her to clothe herself with fine linen, bright and pure" (Revelation 19:7-8). As one who belongs to the Bride of Christ, the wonder of that wedding day is yours—yours to anticipate, yours to savour, yours to hold onto in the darkest night.

It may be that you are tempted to envy your married friends for the happy companionship they enjoy (but you don't), the physical delights of intimacy that are theirs (but not yours), the security of being a couple (unlike the challenges you face of walking alone). But remember this: the joy of your wedding day will eclipse the very best of any human marriage. On that day there will be a fellowship far deeper than that of the fondest couple in this age, a release and ecstasy far better than the happiest love-making on earth, and a security much greater than any that the promises of human marriage provide. You have no need to envy anything—anything!—that married friends may have now.

2. STRENGTHEN THE MARRIAGES OF OTHERS

And therefore, when God calls you to support, to pray for, and to do what you can to strengthen the marriages of others, you can do it. "Oh," you say, "that sounds hard and rather miserable. What can there possibly be in it for me?" And yet, of course, as soon as you ask that question, you put it into the sunlight of God's truth, and you know it's the wrong question. The will of God is always good. What can there be not to like about being faithful to Jesus, about demonstrating loving obedience to God? If this is what God calls me to, I may rest confident that God will enable me to learn a glad contentment in doing it.

And so you can gladly commit yourself to doing what you can to support the marriages of others. You can pray specifically for particular couples in your church at this stage of life. An unmarried woman can be the kind of friend to a married woman who encourages her not to grumble, to be patient in difficult days, to learn to love her sometimes unlovable husband and so on. You can be the kind of friend who does not amplify your married friend's complaining ("Oh, you poor thing; that does sound so unfair...") but points her to the promises of the gospel and God's call to thankful faithfulness.[6] Likewise an unmarried man may have opportunity to encourage a brother who confides in you some of the frustrations of his marriage. Point him to Jesus and the gospel!

---

6 It is worth being clear that I do not have in mind the evils of abuse here. If you have any concerns in this direction, you should seek advice. You can call the National Domestic Abuse Helpline on 0808 2000 247 (UK) or the National Domestic Violence Hotline on 1.800.799.7233 (USA). Your pastor should also be able to advise you.

3. FLEE SEXUAL IMMORALITY

Sexual temptation is live and active for unmarried Christians in their fifties and sixties. Take great care not to stir up sexual desires and passions by what you watch or read. Guard the boundaries of marriages so that you do not transgress the clear command of the Lord Jesus: "What … God has joined together, let not man separate" (Matthew 19:6). Don't drift into emotional dependence or inappropriate non-physical intimacy with a married man or woman. Men, I think it wise not to enter the home of a married woman while her husband is away and no one else is present; and similarly for women with the home of a married man.

4. PRAY TO LEARN CONTENTMENT

If this is an area where you find yourself thinking, "If only", pray to learn to accept your circumstances as the gift of God to you for this time of your life, much as Paul commends in 1 Corinthians 7:7. Say to the God who loves and cares for you, "Lord, I wish I was happily married; I do not know why you have chosen not to give me this gift, but I take my present unmarried state as a gift given me from my loving Father's hand". And indeed, those who are happily and contentedly unmarried can happily and contentedly thank the Father for this gift!

5. BE WISE IF YOU HAVE THE OPPORTUNITY TO MARRY

It is worth mentioning that it is not altogether uncommon to have the opportunity to marry in this stage of life, or perhaps to marry again. This short book is not the place to give pastoral advice about this. But it is worth saying that such an opportunity needs to be weighed up very carefully, not least to be sure that it falls within the will of God. You will do well to ask the counsel of your pastors and others who know you well and have your best interests at heart (see 1 Corinthians 7:39-40). Marriage may be God's way for you, and there may be great vistas of married contentment just over the horizon. But it is not always so. It may be easier to learn contentment unmarried, much as our culture may think this absurd.

To Those Who Are Married

Now let me turn to those of us who are married during this season of life. How can we make our marriages clearer and brighter images of the marriage of Christ and his church? For these are years of glorious possibilities, and perhaps especially during times of trial.

1. INTENTIONALLY STRENGTHEN YOUR MARRIAGE

If your marriage has been generally steady and happy, it is all too easy to coast—just to assume things will chug along cheerfully. They may, or they may not. This is a good time to think together about how things are changing, perhaps in some of the ways opened up by this little book. For example, if you have children who are leaving home, how can you adapt your patterns of married life to make sure you work together through these big changes? When the nest begins to empty, the new space in the home can reveal deeper things than dusty bedrooms; maybe you have been so focused on bringing up the children that you have neglected your marriage. This would be a good time to put that right. Retirement and care for elderly parents can likewise disrupt established patterns of relating to one another.

If you have less time than you once did, how will you guard time for enjoying one another's company and keeping your friendship rich? If you have perhaps a little more time, how can you invest some of this in the friendship and companionship of marriage? Husbands, what does it mean to love our wives "in an understanding way" (1 Peter 3:7), walking with them through what may be huge changes in their bodies (see "menopause" appendix) and the families they have nurtured for so long? Wives, how can you make sure you love and care for your husbands as they, too, walk through times of change? The answers to all these questions will be different for every couple. But I want to encourage you to be deliberate and thoughtful about making these decades a time of enriched and deepened marriage.

One of the longest-lasting joys of married life is the comfort of a close friendship that just goes on and on through the years. For some this comes very naturally; their marriages are built on natural friendship and have been since the beginning. Others have to work harder at this. Spend time together developing shared interests that pull your attention outwards towards the wonders of God's world and the creativity of his image-bearers. Read a book or listen to a podcast together. Go on expeditions and adventures. Keep having fun!

2. BE DELIBERATE IN SERVING THE LORD TOGETHER

Remember, you are not married primarily for your own happiness and satisfaction. You are married so that you may serve God as a couple, just as we are to serve God when unmarried. It is just that there will be differences in how we serve God. But look outwards. In the language of Genesis 2, there is a garden to be looked after, and we are to do this together (Genesis 2:15, 18).

So perhaps reread chapter 4 together and make some bold plans to serve Jesus and his gospel together in fresh ways. This is not a substitute for deepening your friendship and intimacy, but it will prove a healthy and life-giving overflow from that heart of married love.

For some, there will be rich openings to encourage younger married couples in the Lord, not because you necessarily have vast stores of wisdom (!) but simply because you have been around the being-married block a few more times than them. Likewise there will be opportunities to provide companionship for single friends and point them to Jesus.

For others, reading this is painful because your spouse is not following Jesus. Perhaps they have never professed faith; or perhaps they were as zealous as you once but have drifted away over the years. For a wife, it was to women in your situation that Peter spoke of "the imperishable beauty of a gentle and quiet spirit, which in God's sight is very precious" (1 Peter 3:4). So, whether you are a husband with an unbelieving wife or a wife with an unbelieving husband, know that the Lord sees you, that he understands how it feels to be pulled in two directions, and that he delights to see you seeking to walk in obedience, as best as you can in your circumstances. And know that you do not walk alone, however much you may feel that you do. The Spirit walks with you—to every service, to every Bible study, and in every moment at home. Do not think that your service of the Lord Jesus is somehow less than that of friends with a believing spouse. Your believing spirit and faithful discipleship, and your love for your wife or husband, is very precious in God's sight.

3. NOURISH INTIMACY IN YOUR MARRIAGE

For most of us, our fifties and sixties are a time when the fires of passion that raged in our teens and twenties are gradually metamorphosing into something less tumultuous. Well, sometimes. There will come a time, if we live into old age, when—in the language of that most poignant poem in Ecclesiastes 12—"desire fails" (v 5). But in the afternoon of life that time is not yet. Desire—both sexual desire and all the accompanying longings for married happiness, often experienced in different ways by men and women—yet lives.

Sexual intimacy within marriage is a gift from God. In 1 Corinthians 7:1-6 Paul says that it is good for one man to have one woman in marriage and, within that covenant relationship, for each to give themselves to the other freely and gladly. That is to say, there is apostolic authority for nourishing the sexual relationship within marriage. Even as our bodies begin to age, there can be great comfort and joy in knowing that each is giving to the other all that they are. Do not take one another for granted, and do not assume that a healthy intimacy will just happen. Life is busy. So take care to guard time and space for the intimacy at the heart of a healthy marriage to thrive. This intimacy is far more than physical—and some of us need reminding of that—but it is not less.

4. FLEE FROM SEXUAL IMMORALITY

That said, this is sometimes easier said than done. There are a thousand and one reasons why one spouse may disappoint the other through no fault of their own. The desire of a wife and the desire of a husband do not always slow down in happy pace with one another. Sickness, surgery, mental-health struggles and many other things can take away desire and enjoyment from a husband or wife. Dare I say it, there are all sorts of reasons why things simply don't "work" like they perhaps used to in our twenties or thirties. A wife's responses, a husband's arousal—all these things can begin to malfunction; and sometimes this begins during our fifties and sixties. When this happens, we must continue patiently and graciously to bear with one another—and be alert to the temptation to find sexual satisfaction outside of the marriage bed. It is to this second area which we now turn.

First, at the most simple level, we take extra care to keep healthy boundaries in place. Where such boundaries lie will depend on a clear-eyed assessment of the dangers for you in your circumstances and will be decided in conversation with your spouse. For my part, I have operated on the principle that a wise husband will simply not have a woman other than his wife in his home when his wife is absent—and vice versa. I have taken great care to ensure that when I meet one to one with a member of the opposite sex, I meet in public places. Once you have decided where your boundaries lie, be vigilant about keeping them. The devil will whisper, "Just this time I'm sure you can make an exception". Don't. You will regret it. Guard these simple boundaries.

Second—and more subtly—we will be careful not to be sucked into emotional dependence or an inappropriate closeness with a member of the opposite sex. The scenario of the successful man with a distracted wife but an attentive PA who gazes admiringly at him and hangs on his every word is a cliché; but it is a cliché based on patterns all too familiar to us. And it's not simply the successful man who may be drawn—oh, so gradually and understandably—into an emotional dependence that can grow wings and cross the boundaries of the marriage bed. A woman in her fifties or sixties, perhaps disappointed or frustrated in marriage, can easily find herself magnetically drawn to a man other than her husband: a man who seems so much better a listener—a sympathetic shoulder that becomes much more. Be careful. Do not assume that you alone in the human race are immune to such temptations.

One way to fight such temptations is to be realistic about the shame and misery that will result if we fall into sin in this area. As a friend of mine said, "I cannot face the thought of having to tell my grandchildren that I decided not to be faithful to the wife of my youth—that

I chose to break my vows to her. Somehow, as I see their trusting faces, the excuses I want to make evaporate into the insubstantial vapour that they are." The devil always paints sexual sin in shining bright colours to disguise the ugly reality underneath. It doesn't take long for the devil's whitewash to evaporate; and then we will have to face and live with the ugly misery that we have caused.

Finally, be very careful with your eyes: what or who you look at. I doubt I am the only man who has struggled with the ever present temptations of watching things I ought not to watch. While pornography is particularly destructive, there are many things not so classified that stir up a desire in us that is immoral—whether that is a scene in a film, words on a page, or an attractive person scantily dressed on a hot summer's day. Be careful. You cannot perhaps help the first look. But it is often with the second look, the look that lingers, that the danger lies. Pray for the self-control to look away. And in the latter case, perhaps also—as an older never-married friend once said to me—say a quick prayer simply to thank God for making a lovely woman or a good-looking man. And then leave it at that.

5. DEVELOP FRIENDSHIPS THAT STRENGTHEN MARRIAGE

It is also possible to develop friends of the same sex with whom you can share appropriately and pray about your marriages. My fellow husbands, good friendships with men—such as three or four men meeting for prayer—can be a great help in keeping us growing in this area. Let us help one another. In my experience, Christian women are often streets ahead of us men in such wholesome encouragement of one another! We must be careful not to betray confidences, but it is no bad thing to admit to one another that we need God's help as husbands or wives.

The Marriage Supper of the Lamb

Let me close by saying again the most important thing in this whole chapter, to both marrieds and unmarrieds: keep your sights on the marriage supper of the Lamb! Whoever you are and whatever your circumstances, remember that if you belong to Jesus Christ, you are a member of his beloved Bride. And therefore there is in store for you—for all of us in Christ—a wedding day that will put all human wedding days into the shade. The most joyful marriage on earth, the most satisfying sex in history, the most comforting married companionship in this life, will all pale into insignificance beside the glorious joy of Jesus' wedding day. On that day, every godly longing of the human heart will be most wonderfully fulfilled and superseded. And if my heart is filled with this prospect, all my natural longings regarding marriage in this age will lose their intensity, and temptations of all kinds will lose their pull.

So look forward to Jesus' wedding day! For that is your and my wedding day. And what a day that will be!

Questions and Responses

1. Bring into the open before God the "if onlys" of your life. Place them, as it were, on the table and shine the light of God's wisdom, love and power upon them. Then throw them away and do not let them creep back out of the rubbish bin!

2. What are the sadnesses and frustrations for you in this stage of life, so far as marriage is concerned? Bring these into the open before God. Ask him to help you to grow contentment whatever your circumstances.

3. What are the (married or unmarried) joys for you at this stage of life? Thank God for them.

4. If you are married, consider if there are particular ways, now at this stage of life, in which you can guard and nourish your marriage.

5. Likewise, if you are unmarried, ponder how you can strengthen and protect the marriages of married couples known to you.

6. Spend some time meditating on the wedding day of Jesus our Bridegroom and us, his Bride. Rejoice. Let this gladden your heart. Seek to grow the spiritual discipline of turning your thoughts to this when the sadnesses of life crowd in.

Karen and Pete were having a grandparent-ish chat with Clare and Ola. Both couples were in their late fifties and had begun to have grandchildren in different parts of the country.

Karen and Pete were saying that their daughter and son-in-law were hoping they could come over for a day a week to help with childcare, as they were both in full-time employment.

Clare and Ola hadn't felt they had the time or energy to do that when their son had asked them, although they felt a bit bad about that.

Both couples were grappling not only with what to do or not do but also with feeling bad about whatever decisions they made.

Chapter 7

Younger Family

One generation shall commend your works to another, and shall declare your mighty acts.

Psalm 145:4

Before I say a little about the questions that Karen, Pete, Clare and Ola faced, I want to raise our eyes to a bigger vision. This is a vision that all of us are part of—whether or not we have children of our own.

Because we all grow old and die, the church of God will only continue if one generation commends God's great works to another and the younger generation believes. These "works" encompass God's power and majesty as Creator, and his love and faithfulness as Redeemer. They include all the marvellous beauty of God: Father, Son and Holy Spirit. As Psalm 78 sings, we "tell to the coming generation the glorious deeds of the LORD, and his might, and the wonders that he has done," so that "the next generation might know" these things, but they also will "arise and tell them to their children" (v 4-8). And on and on.

When this does not happen, disaster ensues for the church. During the days of Joshua, and even of "the elders who outlived Joshua", the people served the Lord, because these "had seen all the great work that the LORD had done for Israel". But then, when "all that generation" had died, "there arose another generation after them who did not know the LORD or the work that he had done for Israel" (Judges 2:7-10). And so they turned away from believing and obeying. This miserable pattern of unbelief dominates the book of Judges. And it is very dark.

In glorious contrast to these dark shadows, the vision of a faithful church from generation to generation is seen again and again in the Psalms. In the prophecy of the vindicated Messiah that closes Psalm 22, we read that "Posterity shall serve [the Messiah]; it shall be told of the Lord to the coming generation; they shall come and proclaim his righteousness to a people yet unborn" (v 30-31). Believers are exhorted in Psalm 48 to ponder all that is signified by the towers and ramparts of Jerusalem so "that you may tell the next generation that this is God, our God for ever and ever" (v 13-14). In Psalm 71 the psalmist prays that he may live to "proclaim your might to another generation, your power to all those to come" (v 18). And we see similar things in Psalm 79 ("from generation to generation we will recount your praise", v 13); Psalm 89 ("with my mouth I will make known your faithfulness to all generations", v 1); and Psalm 102

("Let this be recorded for a generation to come, so that a people yet to be created may praise the LORD", v 18).

The purpose of this chapter is to explore what it means to live through your fifties and sixties enthused by this idea of faithfulness rolling on through the generations. Each of us will only be around for a mere few decades; in one sense the best we can hope for is, like David, to serve the purpose of God in our own generation (Acts 13:36). And yet, how wonderful to also be part of this great chain of faithfulness in which the baton is picked up by the next generation, and then the next, and the next, until the Lord returns.

We see this in beautiful microcosm in the faith that dwelt in Timothy's grandmother Lois, and his mother, Eunice, and then in Timothy himself (2 Timothy 1:5). Proverbs speaks of leaving an "inheritance" for one's children's children (Proverbs 13:22); although presumably this includes a financial inheritance, I hope we can think more broadly about the rich inheritance that believers can leave to their younger family in other ways.

I have expressed this vision—as the Psalms do—in terms of one generation and another. By this, I mean to direct our attention not simply to the immediate biological children, and then grandchildren, of a father and a mother. I want you to hold in your mind a broader picture that includes, for example, adoptive and step-children, nephews and nieces, godchildren (in traditions that have them), and all sorts of other younger people to whom any of us can become father figures or mother figures, and then grandfatherly or grandmotherly figures. So please read "generation" in this broad sense. This vision includes you if, for example, you have never married or are married but without children. You too can be a shining part of this relay race of faith. And of course there is another direction for us to look in. A friend in his early seventies tells me he is going to visit a believer in his nineties to ask him for his wisdom about living through this next decade. Even in our fifties and sixties, we must not forget what the older generations can teach us.

I'm conscious that parents reading this will be in a variety of family circumstances. Perhaps you have a son or daughter who is adult in years but still significantly dependent upon you, whether emotionally or financially or both. Some will still be living in the parental home. That will greatly affect a godly perspective on how to love them. Some adult sons and daughters are following the Lord; others are not. Some have children, some do not. And, for so many of us in this broken world, there are the great complexities and perplexities of fractured and sometimes reconstituted or "blended" families. The pain of a son or daughter's marriage break-up is like a dagger in a parent's heart. You would not wish this on anyone, it hurts so much. But God's grace is sufficient—and it can shine light into hearts in our most broken of families. Nevertheless, because our circumstances are so very varied, I will major on scriptural principles and say relatively little about the infinite variety of practicalities.

Principles of Inter-Generational Faithfulness

If this chapter is illuminated by one bright vision—of a church faithful from generation to generation until the Lord returns—it is driven by one very simple principle, in two parts: the generation that passes on the baton of faith does so, first, by seeing and believing the works of God for themselves and then by speaking these words with joy to the next generation. Although we may be tempted to jump to the second of these (the speaking), I want to encourage you to think about the all following elements.

LONG AND PRAY FOR GOD TO GIVE SPIRITUAL LIFE

When we rightly behold the wonderful works of God in creation and redemption, we will bow before the sovereignty of God in all things. And, in particular, in the matter of faith.

No child follows the Lord except by a supernatural work of God in his or her heart. No child becomes a lifelong follower of Jesus because their parents were good parents; and conversely, when God works in a person's life, the worst parenting in the world and the most deeply broken family will not stop them being born again.

There is no sadder experience for a parent than to watch a daughter or son turn away from the Lord. There are many things we yearn for our children, but none come close to this: like Paul with his Jewish brethren, our "heart's desire and prayer to God for them is that they may be saved" (Romans 10:1). When we see our children choose not to believe, it nearly breaks our hearts.

And yet, to bow in adoring worship before the wise sovereignty of our good God brings comfort and drives us to our knees in prayer. I know friends who have a special list of prodigals in their prayers, to which they add the names of youngsters who have turned away. For myself, one of the things that most moves me is to hear a friend, perhaps a friend I have not been in touch with for years, say, "I am still praying for..."—and then to name an unbelieving member of my own family. God sees. God knows. God counts a parent's tears and puts them in his bottle (Psalm 56:8).

SET AN EXAMPLE OF FAITH AND GODLINESS

A believer in her fifties and sixties will take especial care to set an example of faith and godliness. Every believer of any age ought to do this, of course. But there is perhaps a particular weight that attaches to a Christian in this afternoon of life. Sons and daughters—whether your own or those of your peers—are often reaching that transitional age when they are beginning to cut the apron strings and make their own way in a very confusing world. Yet as they move into adulthood, they still watch, they observe keenly, they wonder. No longer do they assume that "mummy and daddy are always right". Now they watch with the critical eyes of a young adult. And what they see in their homes and among more senior adults will be at least as influential for them as what they may hear by way of explicit Christian teaching.

They will see, for example, if Christian parents and other adults acknowledge their failings and ask for forgiveness. They watch to see if we are filled with thankfulness or whether perhaps we default to grumbling and complaining. They listen to hear if we speak well of people or if we gossip and do people down behind their backs. They may hear words of Christian commitment, but they look to see if these are lived out in lives of worship, obedience and adoration of God—or if perhaps there are clear idolatries, perhaps of career or pleasure or popularity. They observe our topics of conversation and they learn what gets us out of bed in the morning and gives us joy. They gaze, day after day, at indicators of what is going on in our hearts.

So let us long and pray that they will see in our homes the fruit of the Spirit; that they will watch us persevere in difficult days; that they will witness faithfulness in our marriages—ultimately, that they will have placarded before their eyes lives lived in the presence of God.

BE INTENTIONAL ABOUT MAINTAINING RELATIONSHIPS WITH YOUNGER GENERATIONS

A believer in the afternoon of life will be wise to prioritise, and to work intentionally at, maintaining relationships with the younger generation. This is most obviously true for parents of teenagers. But it is also applicable to mums and dads of young-adult sons and daughters, even—perhaps especially—when they are not following the Lord.

It is, I think, helpful for parents to remember that their calling is to be parents. That sounds obvious, so let me explain what I mean. A mum or a dad is not the pastor of their son or daughter or even the evangelist. A mother is to be a mother and to maintain that motherly relationship as her sons and daughters grow. A father is to be a father. It seems to me that some of the difficulties in Christian homes can be exacerbated when a parent (perhaps especially a father) defaults to behaving like an evangelist or a pastor to his errant or difficult son or daughter. If that is your tendency, beware: you are called to be his or her father. You are to be there as a dad. And that relationship continues until you die. It is therefore of the highest significance to guard and nourish those relationships—and similarly for uncles and aunts and other motherly or fatherly relationships.

When, as is so often the case, the younger generation includes broken marriages or "blended families", it is easy to underestimate the power of simply being there as a stable presence amid the chaos of life. It may be not so much what I say or do that has the impact as simply the fact that I am there—steadily there—as mother, father, grandparent, uncle or aunt, and so on.

For those whose sons or daughters are married, there is the additional opportunity (and sometimes challenge) of relating to a son-in-law or daughter-in-law. How wonderful to have this opening to care in a family context for a new person in the image of God! And yet it can be difficult, as the plethora of mother-in-law jokes attests (although I suspect that fathers-in-law like me cause at least as many problems). We will be realistic about the challenges. But we will be willing to devote energy and time to building these relationships as well as we can, and repairing them when there are hurts.

LET THEM KNOW THAT YOU ARE ON THEIR SIDE

Look for ways to signal to the younger generation that you are on their side, that you are for them, and that you want the best for each of them. How you do that will depend on many factors, not least how close you live (or if they still live in the home), your own age and state of health and strength, and your and their circumstances.

For many this will involve a generosity in passing on financial help as and when you are able to do so. It is a winsome thing when a senior generation do not lavish their spare money on selfish pleasures but rather do what they can to support the younger generation as they seek to make their way in life. For some of us in good health and who live nearby, there may be all manner of practical ways in which we can offer to help, especially as our offspring set out on the adventures of parenthood. It is not uncommon in Western cultures for grandparents (typically) to give substantial practical assistance to young parents, although there can be a downside to this if it stops the older generation being present where they live and really belonging to their church (see chapter 8).

These practical decisions need to be made with great care. We must not simply let cultural expectations pressure us into conformity.

SEEK OPPORTUNITIES TO GIVE TESTIMONY TO YOUNGER GENERATIONS

In these four ways—and perhaps others—"afternooners" can demonstrate that they are those who have seen and known in their own experience the wonderful works of God. It is on the basis of this—this submission to God's sovereignty, godly example of faith, commitment to relationship, and being on their side—that we may then hope to speak to the next generation of God as Creator and Redeemer, as the Psalms celebrate.

Of course, our speaking alone will be insufficient to pass on the baton of faith. The younger generation need to listen! As we have thought earlier, only a supernatural work of the Spirit of God will enable them to do so.

The interplay between speaking and listening can be complex. In the very simplest, and best, scenario, Christian afternooners enjoy an open door to speak freely about the faith, and the younger generation are eager to listen. When an edifying book is given, it is read eagerly and gladly. When a word of biblical wisdom is spoken, it is heard with open ears. Godly advice is sought and heeded.

In particular, we will communicate our values by our congratulations. If we say that our Christian faith matters most to us, but we rejoice most audibly in their examination successes, their sporting triumphs, their career progression, their relationships and so on, then we contradict our profession with our congratulations. Oh, sure, we will be glad when we hear of these other successes. But somehow we will communicate that what gives us most joy is their faith and godliness. We will take especial care that they notice how pleased we are when we see them persevere in times of disappointment and trial.

And yet I hear some say under their breath, "I wish! Oh, how I wish this were me." What if they won't listen to words of faith? What then?

There may be an analogy with the Christian wife who has an unbelieving husband, addressed by Peter in 1 Peter 3:1-2. Peter sets before her the hope that her husband may be "won without a word" as he sees the godly life of his wife. I take it this does not mean that this husband never hears the word of the gospel, but rather that he does not hear it repeatedly and irritatingly from his wife. She grasps that she is his wife and not his preacher! In a somewhat similar way, it is wise for the afternoon generation not to nag, not to pester, not to sound like a cracked record, not constantly to speak of Christ from the metaphorical soapbox but rather to pray for opportunities to slip in a word of testimony or a phrase about Christ. When younger ones are in our homes we may, I think, very reasonably say a prayer of thanksgiving before a meal. At any time, when asked how we are, we may include in our answer something about how kind God has been to us and how grateful we are for our sins to be forgiven. There are very natural ways to do this—ways that are not "preachy" but simply the overflow of our lives.

It is also possible—although I suspect this is less common—for an open-eared younger generation to be starved of life-giving words because the afternooners in their lives are reluctant to speak or frightened of giving offence or just plain lazy. I know I have been guilty in all these ways, and I need to repent. Perhaps as you finish this chapter, you could ask the Lord to give you fresh hope in his gracious power to save and fresh resolve to speak life-giving words to the younger generation.

I began this chapter with two imaginary couples—Karen and Pete, and Clare and Ola. I have not attempted to "solve" the puzzles with which they were grappling. But I hope that this vision of inter-generational faithfulness will shine light on their conversation. I hope all grandparents—indeed, all Christians—will long most eagerly to see faith passed down, to be shining examples of godly living, to work hard at maintaining supportive relationships with younger generations, and to look for opportunities to bear winsome testimony to God's grace in Jesus.

Questions and Responses

1. Whatever your circumstances, begin by bringing before the Lord the younger generations in your life, even—perhaps especially—in all their brokenness. Do not be afraid to weep in your prayers for them. But keep your eyes on the God of infinite kindness and grace.

2. How can you make sure that the example you set to younger generations is supremely one of faith and godliness? Are there areas where you are aware you need to change?

3. Which relationships with younger generations are easy and which are difficult? Are there actions you can take to move the difficult ones in a better direction? Are you in danger of drifting away from some precisely because they are difficult? How can you avoid doing that?

4. How can you express to the younger generations in your life that you truly are on their side—that you want God's best for them?

5. What opportunities do you have to speak words of testimony to younger generations in your life?

The pastor remembers Tom and Emma in their mid-twenties, when they ran the youth group. They were newly married and were a beacon of humble, faithful dedication in this ministry. They worked so hard week after week. When they had children, they moved to leading and hosting a small group in their home. And then, in their forties, the pastor urged them to take a break, not least because their then teenage youngsters needed a lot of attention.

Tom and Emma are in their early fifties now. Their teenagers are now adults and have left home. But to his sadness, the pastor realises that Tom and Emma have drifted out of any form of service in church. Probably one Sunday in three—or even every other week—they simply aren't there at all.

Chapter 8

Church

So then you are no longer strangers and aliens, but you are fellow citizens with the saints and members of the household of God, built on the foundation of the apostles and prophets, Christ Jesus himself being the cornerstone, in whom the whole structure, being joined together, grows into a holy temple in the Lord. In him you also are being built together into a dwelling place for God by the Spirit.

Ephesians 2:19-22

I want in this chapter to exhort you to belong to an imperfect local church. Not simply to attend but to belong. It may be that you were deeply committed to one or more local churches earlier in your life, like Tom and Emma. You have understood God's vision and purpose for the church. And yet, at this stage of life, it is all too easy to lose this first love and to do church lightly—to attend from time to time, sure, but no longer deeply to belong. So let me try to fire you afresh with a vision for the local church.

A Vision for the Local Church

Some years ago I wrote a book that told the story of the whole Bible themed around scattering (as a sign of God's judgment) and gathering (the work of God's grace). I called it *Remaking a Broken World*. Seldom have I so enjoyed the studies of Scripture than those that fed into that Bible overview. Let me just give you three highlights—three reasons to stir you to commit yourself to the local church in this window of your life.

THE CHURCH IS A PLACE OF RECONCILIATION

We live in a deeply broken world, riven with strife and ruined by discord on every level—from marriages and personal relationships right up to international affairs. What hope is there for such a world? It is all very well for people to tell us that we ought to try harder to get along. We know that. What we need is a power working within each of us that will enable us to begin to do that. This power is found in the crucified Christ. The passage at the start of the chapter from Paul's letter to the church in Ephesus speaks much about how the gospel brings together men and women separated by one of the deepest divides in ancient society, that between Jew and Gentile. They are both—Jew and Gentile—reconciled to God through the cross of Christ (Ephesians 2:16).

This sounds very wonderful. But where is it seen in actual human life? It is known and experienced in a healthy local church. This is the place where men and women, young and old, rich and poor, privileged and despised, respectable and disreputable, from every race, ethnicity, culture and nation, are brought together in love as brothers and sisters. Local churches are wonderful places, even though we often fail to see this.

THE CHURCH IS WHERE GOD DWELLS ON EARTH

The second highlight is that the church is where God dwells on earth today. Paul calls it "a holy temple", "a dwelling place for God by the Spirit" (v 21-22). If you want to see the invisible God, you cannot physically see Jesus now because he is risen and ascended. But you can see and experience the society in which God lives by the Spirit of Jesus. There is no place like it on earth—just as, under the old covenant, there was no place like the temple on earth.

THE CHURCH IS AN ARROW OF HOPE TO THE FUTURE

The third reason to commit to the local church is because it is an arrow of hope to the future—a taste of the heavenly Jerusalem, which the earthly Jerusalem of the Bible foreshadows.

The name "Jerusalem" means the city of peace (see Psalm 122). Jerusalem in the Middle East is anything but a city of peace. But the local church, the temple of the living God, is a kind of Jerusalem on earth (albeit always mixed with something of "Babylon", the city of discord). It points to the true Jerusalem, which will come down from heaven to earth on the last day and form the new creation, drawing together all the church of Christ in every age (Revelation 21). When you and I belong to a local church, we breathe an anticipatory fragrance of the beauty of the new Jerusalem. Imperfect as they are, local churches in which the word of God is faithfully taught are places that contain the DNA of a remade world.

It may well be that the most significant thing you do in your life is truly to belong to a local church. In it you are part of God remaking a broken world. In it you enjoy the presence of God on earth. And in it you are a pointer of hope to the culmination of human history. Surely that is sufficient reason to commit yourself in this "not old, not young" stage of life to a local church!

Three Warnings to Heed

So what does this look like in practice? First, I want to set out three warnings to heed—temptations with peculiar traction at just this stage of life. Then I will close with four positives.

WARNING 1: BEWARE NOT LIVING WHERE YOU LIVE (ESPECIALLY ON SUNDAYS)

My first warning is a strangely first-world caution. Many of our young people attend a college or university away from home—perhaps a long way away. Their roots at home are damaged or even pulled up. Perhaps they then move to live in another part of the country—or even in another country altogether. As they do so, their parents—and perhaps wider family—begin to feel a pull away from where they live. There are beloved children, or nephews and nieces, and later perhaps grandchildren, to visit, some distance away. Sometimes of course these dear ones come to see us. But often we afternooners need to be the ones who take the initiative to go and visit them.

What happens then? While we are in paid employment, we cannot visit them during the week except by taking some of our precious annual-leave allowance. It is therefore natural to plan our visits at weekends. And it doesn't take long before our attendance at our own church becomes sporadic, erratic and infrequent. It is astonishing how quickly this can happen. You may find it helpful to go through your calendar for the past twelve months and see how many of the 52 Sundays saw you away from home. Perhaps every absence was for a good and justifiable reason—a special birthday, an anniversary, a graduation and so on. But watch the sum total. Are you beginning not to live where you live, at least so far as Sundays are concerned?

Between us missing a Sunday and others missing other Sundays, it can be weeks before we see a particular person again in church. Just as we sometimes write on an envelope that drops through our letter box, "Not known at this address", so we may find that our pastor is beginning to think, "Scarcely known in this church". So think carefully about how to make Sunday a priority for your local church. When people in their fifties and sixties become the absent generation, a church is much the poorer.

Our absences aren't always family-related. Sometimes entirely legitimate pleasures can eat away at church belonging too—travel, adventurous trekking, hobbies, sport or art. All are good gifts our heavenly Father lavishes on us (1 Timothy 6:17). All can be enjoyable. But if they mean I can't belong deeply to my church fellowship, the cost is very high. Ungodliness can creep in on the shoulders of legitimate pleasures.

WARNING 2: TAKE CARE NOT TO DRIFT OUT OF SERVING

My second warning overlaps with the first. Take care that you do not grow weary in doing good—that you do not say to yourself (or to others), "You know, I have served a lot, and I am weary; I feel I have done my bit for the church and the gospel."

Now let me qualify this. We do grow weary. There is a sabbatical principle in Scripture. There are times and seasons to take a break, as Tom and Emma needed to do.

What I am warning against is an attitude that says this: "I think I have done enough. Period. I have served in my twenties, thirties, and forties. And now it is time to put down my pack and rest." And rest. And rest. And never pick up the pack and serve again. That can happen by drift rather than by crisis. I take a break—perhaps a necessary break. And then somehow the break goes on and on. Other things come in to fill up my time and use my energy. And serving in church has drifted down into the "maybe later" (or "maybe not at all") category in the basement of my priorities list.

WARNING 3: DON'T BECOME A GRUMBLER

My third warning is somewhat different. It is a warning

for those who *are* in church Sunday by Sunday, who *are* committed, who serve, who give of themselves sacrificially, who are thoroughly involved. And it is this: don't become a grumbler. Any of us can grumble at any age. Afternooners have no monopoly on grumbling. But perhaps it is a particularly aggressive temptation in our fifties and sixties—a warm-up act to the main-stage display of grumpiness that can come to characterise old age.

Grumbling is fed by a sense that things are not as they used to be. It looks back to an imagined golden age. Sometimes—paradoxically—a really good experience under the leadership of a fine pastor of yesteryear can become a seed for complaining later under a different leader. "It wasn't like this in so-and-so's day," we say. The preaching isn't what it used to be. The music has deteriorated, in content or quality. There is a lack of vision or imaginative outreach. And so on. And so nostalgia segues into grumbling.

Eventually we become the most miserable of people. You can spot us in church, usually off to one side, having a (fairly) discreet mutter with one or two who will go along with our mutterings and even amplify them ("I couldn't agree more. Yes, you're right. And then there's this as well…"). Festering discontent attaches itself to us like iron filings to a magnet. Don't become like this! Don't grumble.

Four Bright Ambitions

So after those three warnings, let me turn to four bright ways forward.

1. LOOK FOR FRESH OPPORTUNITIES TO SERVE IN YOUR LOCAL CHURCH

If church really is the most significant thing God is doing in the world—a beacon of reconciliation, the dwelling place of God, a community that contains the DNA of the new creation—then we will gladly pour our energies into it. As Paul writes, "Do not be slothful in zeal, be fervent in spirit, serve the Lord" (Romans 12:11). While there is life, always there are good works prepared beforehand for you to walk in, if you belong to Jesus Christ (Ephesians 2:10). So look for them. And look for them in your local church.

Don't be like Diotrephes, who just loved to be first and was always pushing himself to the front (3 John 1:9). There are ministries in church life which are filled by the elders and leaders after prayer; if they ask you to consider such a ministry, take their approach very seriously. By all means pray for openings to do such things. But don't expect them, even if you have done them in the past.

But there are plenty of things for which it is entirely appropriate simply to volunteer. Such will include a multiplicity of practical tasks, from the dignity of cleaning and moving chairs through the hard work of cooking or baking for a church event to some skilled professional or semi-professional roles helping with administering finances. Speak to your pastor about these things. Let him know that you desire to serve and are willing to serve in any way you can.

2. CONSIDER IF THIS STAGE OF LIFE GIVES NEW OPPORTUNITIES FOR HOSPITALITY

Perhaps you are unmarried or do not have children. Maybe your children are beginning to be away from home more. One way or another, you may find yourself in your fifties and sixties with sufficient room in your home to exercise hospitality in a way you have perhaps not been able to do in the past. Use these opportunities while you have the energy, the space and the skill. (And, if necessary, try to learn a few culinary skills, as I am belatedly trying to do!) Do not undervalue the blessing that opening your home can be in the life of a church. Look out for those on the edge as well as those in the core of church life. Keep an eye open for newcomers.

3. THINK HOW YOU CAN SUPPORT YOUR CHURCH LEADERS

Let your leaders keep watch over you "with joy" writes the author of Hebrews (13:17). When I left paid pastoral ministry, I began to reflect on how best church members can make their pastor's life a joy rather than a wearisome burden. Because there was no danger people would think I was telling them how to look after me (because I was no longer paid and supported) and by reason of having had overwhelmingly good experiences myself (so I had no axe to grind), I jotted these thoughts down in a little book somewhat mischievously entitled *The Book Your Pastor Wishes You Would Read (But Is Too Embarrassed to Ask)*. It might help you think about how you can support your pastor and elders better.

4. SHARE BIBLICAL WISDOM WITH YOUNGER GENERATIONS IN CHURCH

The teaching of the wise is a fountain of life,
that one may turn away from the snares of death.
(Proverbs 13:14)

It sounds rather grand, even grandiose, to speak of entering a stage of life in which I can share my wisdom with others. "I, who know so much in this afternoon of life, can be for you a fountain of wisdom as I share my riches with you in your poor morning. How blessed you are to know me (and I hope you realise how lucky you are)!" The reality is a lot more humdrum. At the very lowest level, there is a sense in which, just because we have been around the block a few more times, those younger than us can learn from us. We don't need to be on a specially high plane of godly wisdom to be a blessing to those embarking on their early circuits around the blocks of life. And yet wisdom truly is a fountain of life. So let me suggest some simple ingredients for living an afternoon of life in which valuable wisdom is shared with younger believers.

First—and this is easily neglected—try to spend time with younger believers (whether younger in years or younger in faith, or both). Listen to them. Give them time and space to talk. Let trust develop so that they will open up appropriately about what is going on in their hearts.

Second—and I am especially aware of how weak I have been at this—give yourself time to think and pray over what you have heard from a younger believer. It is remarkable, when reading the extraordinary spiritual correspondence of, say, John Newton or Samuel Rutherford, two great pastors from the 17th century, to think how much time and care they spent considering how to counsel those to whom they wrote. For myself, I have often been too preoccupied with my own life to love people enough to give precious time to ponder, to pray, to think, to consider and then to write or to speak with thoughtful counsel.

Third, offering hospitality provides opportunities to share wisdom. So often, when we open the doors of our homes to younger believers, this seems to open doors into their lives. In my experience, godly women, like my lovely wife, do this far better than most of us men. But let's not give up, my fellow men!

Fourth, there may be natural and appropriate opportunities for some of us to take a younger believer under our wings and offer them some kind of mentoring. In his book *Transforming Friendship*, John Wyatt has written movingly about how the late John Stott, former rector of All Souls Church in London, took him under his wing and encouraged him in the life of faith over many years. Wyatt wisely draws careful boundaries in his book, very conscious—as we all must be—of the dangers of abuse. We must be aware that any relationship between an older brother and younger brother, or older sister and younger sister, is a relationship with an inbuilt power imbalance that can be misused by the senior person. Ensure that your relationship is not closeted or cliquey or somehow shrouded in secrecy. But abuse is not inevitable, and there are plenty of shining examples of healthy, natural and profoundly edifying friendships between older and younger believers. If God gives you opportunities during these decades to mentor a younger believer—be that formally or informally—thank God for this and seek to impart wisdom insofar as you are able as you share your life of faith with another. This is a privilege and a joy. Sometimes such friendships may develop out of being asked to do things like marriage preparation. There are many natural and healthy contexts for "afternoon" believers to encourage "morning" believers.

And, while thinking about sharing wisdom with those younger than you, don't forget to mine the wisdom of those older than you! "Wisdom is with the aged, and understanding in length of days" (Job 12:12). Look around in your church. There will very likely be one or another who is frail in body but strong in spirit and rich in wisdom learned over many years. Spend time with them!

Imperfectly Magnificent

Your local church is imperfect. It is probably very ordinary and unimpressive. Your pastor is imperfect. He too may be very ordinary and unimpressive. And yet, to belong to this imperfect but faithful fellowship may be the most significant thing you do with your fifties and sixties. Here is the presence of God on earth. Here God dwells by the Spirit of Christ. Here is the body of Christ. And you—in your fifties and in your sixties—can be a part of this magnificent supernatural work of God upon the earth! Don't miss out on this wonderful privilege.

Questions and Responses

1. Take time out to ponder the majestic significance of the church. Perhaps read through Ephesians with this in mind. Let your heart be filled afresh with a sense of wonder about the very ordinary gatherings each Sunday for worship.

2. How many Sundays were you away from church in the past year? Do an audit of the frequency and the reasons. Review them before God and ask yourself if it would be good to make any changes to your pattern of life.

3. Review conversations you have had recently with your own generation in church. Were there times when you drifted into grumbling? If so, repent, and resolve to be thankful and encouraging.

4. In what ways can you support your church leaders better?

5. What opportunities has God given you to share biblical wisdom with younger believers?

“So, who are you? Tell me about yourself.” Gloria was faced with this question at a party recently. “Well,” she said, “I’m a teacher”. And so the conversation went on.

Alice had the same asked of her. “Oh, me?” she replied. “Well, I do some admin work for a local car-sales business. But really the last couple of decades have just been about being a mother.”

A few days later, Gloria and Alice were chatting after church. Alice was in her fifties—Gloria in her early sixties. They recounted these conversations. And then they began to reflect that each of them had answered a question about identity (“Who are you?”) with an answer about activity (“I am a teacher/mother”). And neither had made any reference to being a Christian. That prompted some soul-searching.

Chapter 9

"Retirement" and Empty-Nesting

The seventy-two returned with joy, saying, "Lord, even the demons are subject to us in your name!" And [Jesus] said to them, "… do not rejoice in this, that the spirits are subject to you, but rejoice that your names are written in heaven."

Luke 10:17-20

For you have died, and your life is hidden with Christ in God.

Colossians 3:3

Cherish your identity in Christ. In this chapter I want to explore some of the questions of identity that swirl around employment and so-called "retirement", and of the beginnings of the "empty nest". Of course, for most in their early fifties, retirement feels a distant horizon. But it creeps up on us faster than we expect, and it is worth thinking about in good time. Actually, I do not think that "retirement" is a helpful word for Christians to use; it can imply that, while I still have health and strength, I can sit back and just enjoy myself! We may stop being paid, but we will not cease to serve Jesus and his gospel. But, since the word is commonly used, I will use it. (I would have liked to have used scare quotes throughout, but my publisher said readers would find it annoying!)

When asked, "Who are you?" many of us, I suspect, answer like Gloria or Alice. We answer as if our questioner had asked, "What do you *do*?" And so we give an activity answer to an identity question: "I *am* a teacher / farm labourer / nurse" (or whatever it may be). Or, perhaps worst of all, "I am *only* a mum" (*only* one of the most significant people in human history!). Although this may seem not to matter, the way we describe ourselves to others shapes how we think. And here's the rub: if I think I *am* what I do, and what I do consists mainly in my paid employment, then, when my paid employment begins to wind down, my whole being feels somehow threatened. Similarly, if I think I *am* what I do in raising children, then, when they leave home, my entire identity is shaken.

This chapter explores some of these questions that revolve around retirement and the empty nest. But let us begin by delighting in our identity in the Lord Jesus Christ. When the disciples came back from their mission trip in Luke 10:17-20 (above), their description of what they had been *doing* was pretty spectacular. It makes even the most shining career or stellar parenting seem dull by comparison. These disciples had exercised the supernatural power of Jesus over demons and all the forces of darkness! And, unsurprisingly, they were very excited about this. Who would not have been? And yet Jesus says to them—in one of his astonishing, loving put-downs!—"Do not rejoice in this". What?! Why not?! Because they should find their joy in something much more fundamental, more precious.

These words from Jesus are so wise. After all, if the disciples' joy and their identity is located in what they do, they are riding for a fall. One day, sooner or later, they will "retire" from casting out demons. One day, perhaps simply through old age, they will do this no more. And their joy will evaporate. They will be tormented by a crisis of identity. And so Jesus says, "Rejoice that your names are written in heaven". *Rejoice that you are my disciples, that you belong to me. You will never lose that.*

And later, after the resurrection and ascension, Paul writes these marvellous words to the Christians in Colossae: "You have died, and your life is hidden with Christ in God" (Colossians 3:3). You live in a body on earth, shadowed by sin and death. But your true identity is in heaven, hidden with the risen and ascended Christ, in the presence of God. Rejoice in this. Live in the light of this. Say this to your own soul again and again. Speak this to one another. Precisely because this is an invisible truth, it can easily become a forgotten truth. And yet it is true: if you are in Christ, you have died, and your life—who you truly are, your identity—is hidden with Christ in God. And nothing can change that. Take care to remember it.

This grand truth is the starting point for all we now consider about work, retirement and empty-nesting. There are three things to do as we contemplate these changes.

Face It

First, it is important to face up to the fact that change will happen. Whatever you are doing at the moment will come to an end.

I was reflecting on a phrase that crops up again and again in 2 Kings, which records the deeds of many of the kings of Judah and Israel. Quite often, the account of each king's reign ends with a similar closing comment: *He did other stuff, and if you want to read up about that, you can find it in this or that chronicle.* (Except that, ironically, you now can't; so all these things the king thought were so important are now lost to history!) *And then he died, and so-and-so (perhaps his son) reigned "in his place".* We skim over these comments. And in some ways it's pretty obvious that someone else will reign in each king's place. But it's powerful, if we stop to think about it. And if it's true for a king, it's true for each of us. Whatever role we may occupy—that job to which we long aspired, this promotion we worked hard to achieve—the time will come when someone else will be doing it *in my place.* Of course they will. But I need to remember that. And most especially when my thoughts are filled by how important I am!

Between us, I'm sure we could tell dozens of anecdotes to illustrate this fact. A friend who had held significant roles in his career told me that when he left his big city workplace, a friend warned him that "the grass grows quickly in [that city]", meaning that things and people change quickly and he will soon be forgotten. The Christian doctor and author Professor John Wyatt often tells the story of how, not long after he retired from a very senior position in charge of a medical unit in central London, he went back for a visit to see how it was all going. A young nurse came up to him—to her, this unknown visitor—and asked if she could help him. And he realised that this was how it was going to be. Very soon he would be forgotten.

I remember visiting a school at which I had held a position of responsibility some years previously. The receptionist had no idea who I was. I had to explain. And that's just how it is. After I had served in one post for a while, they very kindly asked if they could take a portrait photo of me and my wife to hang in some room in their headquarters. And I thought to myself, "This is a sure sign that I am yesterday's man!" I don't even know if the photo is still hanging or if it has been relegated to a dusty cupboard! Because that's how it is. And we need to face up to this. In the moment we can feel we matter—but it won't be long before we don't matter at all.

Something similar happens when it comes to parenting. Our children grow up and, although they don't forget about us and they love us and care for us, they don't need us in the way they once did. And this not-being-needed is hard to get used to. Perhaps someone else takes our place as the most significant person in their life. But we need to face up to it; this is how it will be. When it is hard, remember that your name is written in heaven!

Prepare for It

Second, prepare for it. I am not so much thinking of practical or financial preparations, although these have their place. I mean work on your heart in the presence of God so that you do not rest your identity in your activity, however significant that may seem to you just now. We need to think less about our activity (and how important it is) and a lot more about Christ.

How can we do that? Well, if the language we use of ourselves is a litmus test of how we regard ourselves, then it is also true that changing our language can help us shift our hearts. So why not be radical and give a surprising answer to the request "Tell me about yourself"? "Do you know, you probably weren't asking this, but the most important thing about me is that I am a follower of Jesus Christ." If your conversation partner shows any interest, you can perhaps say more about what it is to belong to Jesus, about the forgiveness of sins, about the Holy Spirit indwelling your heart, about what it means to be in union with Christ in his death and resurrection, and so on. Even if they don't show an interest, you may have sown a seed.

A second way we can help prepare our hearts is actively to encourage the next generation to get ready to step into our shoes. Pray for grace not to resent this but to welcome it—to be genuinely glad as we see them growing in readiness for this. A great by-product of this is that we will not be those tiresome late-afternooners who just hang on and on to our positions (like the phenomenon sometimes known as "bed-blocking").

It may help to conduct a thought experiment. What if tomorrow I am removed from all my roles in life? Perhaps by sudden illness or accident, or maybe by an economic crisis. For whatever reason, I find that all the answers I used to give to the question "Who are you?" no longer apply. How will I feel? If, after the understandable disappointment and shock, I could answer, "Nevertheless, I rejoice that my name is written in heaven, and nothing can change that"—well then, there are signs that my heart is healthy in this regard.

Even so, there is a place for making financial preparations. Be wise about matters such as housing and pensions. But don't be greedy. Do not feel that you have to lay up treasure on earth. Advertisements for pension provision will show models in their healthy forties pretending to be men and women in their sixties, happy because they have laid up amazing treasure for themselves on earth and are therefore able to continue to indulge their selfish pleasures year after year after year. Do not buy into this—a toxic mix of the idolatry of youth and the worship of pleasure. All the same, it is not selfish to make wise provision, if you are able. The purpose of this is that your family or your church will not need to make sacrifices to look after you when a little sensible forethought on your part would have avoided this.

Look Forward to It

Third, look forward to these changes even when they are likely to be some years, or even more than a decade, away. Look forward to the opportunities that God will give: the new good works prepared beforehand that you should walk in them. Dream a little about how you might serve the Lord Jesus with a partly empty nest; turn over in your mind some of the great possibilities for loving the Lord and his gospel after your paid employment comes to an end. The simple act of thinking about possibilities—even if these exact things don't happen—will help you to think of this coming season as one to be welcomed.

But take care that in these daydreams you are not simply wanting to replace one idolatry by another. That you are not looking forward, for example, to some voluntary involvement—perhaps with a charity—as an alternative means to gain status. One of the greatest menaces in voluntary organisations is the men and women who are there because it makes them feel significant. They have lost the significance of paid employment, but now—and what a relief this is to them!—they have status as honorary secretary of this or trustee of that, or whatever it may be. Friends, let's be those who dream dreams about service, not status. Look forward to these possibilities because they give you an honourable and fruitful way to serve Jesus and his gospel.

As retirement or an empty nest draws nearer, you can thank God as each identity marker is stripped away from you, painful as that can often be. Why? Because each tearing off of a spurious identity makes Jesus more precious. Every loss of some cherished source of status presses us back on the wonder of being in Christ. Whatever you have, or have not, achieved in your paid working life, rejoice that your name is written in heaven.

Questions and Responses

1. What answers do you give when someone says, "Tell me about yourself"? Think about an alternative, and then be brave and try it out!

2. Meditate on your identity as a man or woman in Christ. Let your heart sing with wonder.

3. Look back on jobs or occupations you have already finished or left. Face up to the fact that you became "yesterday's man or woman" rather quickly. Let those memories help you face up to what is coming to you if and when you retire.

4. As well as spiritual preparation, are there ways in which you can make wise financial and practical preparations for retirement?

5. What wholesome and gospel-focused things might you look forward to in retirement?

Mike and Ken had known one another as students. Each had been best man at the other's wedding. Their families had kept in touch over the years. Now both in their fifties, they lived some way away from one another. They used to call each other from time to time. But it was hard to meet face to face.

This past week Mike's work had brought him to Ken's town, and so he came to stay. As they reminisced, they realised they had had an amazing amount of shared life over the years. And it was so encouraging for each to hear the other speak about the faithfulness of God to them in the ups and downs of life.

Chapter 10

Friendship

And Jonathan, Saul's son, rose and went to David at Horesh, and strengthened his hand in God.

1 Samuel 23:16

These are … among my fellow workers for the kingdom of God, and they have been a comfort to me.

Colossians 4:11

Why a chapter about friendship? After all, we have friends at all stages of life, not simply in our fifties and sixties. But I think there may be at least two reasons why it is worth revisiting friendship in this "not old, not young" window of life.

First, for many, the realities of marriage and children may mean that once close friendships have drifted apart. We had scores of friends come to our wedding. But, as one child and then perhaps another and another is born, we are so absorbed, taken up and tired by the great project of raising our children that we grow time-poor when it comes to sustaining friendships. And those who remain unmarried or do not have children find themselves frequently on the other end of our time-poverty, so that, although they want to keep up their friendships with us, we struggle to reciprocate. It makes an interesting little study to see how many friends came to your wedding and yet you have never met up with them since. It is a strange paradox that a wedding can be, in this respect, like a funeral; you never see your friends again! No one is necessarily at fault in any of this; it just happens. And so we perhaps find, as we travel through our fifties and sixties, that once precious friendships have gathered dust. Or they are like a beautiful ornament that has become a bit chipped and neglected.

And then there may be a second factor. Many of us move around during our twenties, thirties and forties. Some moves are fairly local, but often our relocations take us to distant cities or other countries. The combination of the busyness of raising a family and the dislocations of house moves can mean that our fifties (or thereabouts) may be a timely moment to think afresh about friendship, and then to act intentionally to rebuild and restore old friendships and to make new ones.

Why Friends?

So let's consider why God gives us friends. Genesis 2:18 is, of course, a text setting the context of marriage: "It is not good that the man should be alone". This is not about the man's loneliness but rather about the need for a helper to work alongside him in the great enterprise of tending God's garden. Man and woman are to work together joyfully to govern God's good world. But, although this text concerns marriage, it flows out into a world full of rich relationships of many kinds. It was never the purpose of God that a human being should walk solo through life. At the very simplest level, we live in a world where there are others around us.

The usual Hebrew word for "friend" is the same as that translated "neighbour" or just "another" human being. But it becomes clear that some of these neighbours mean more to us than simply those who happen to be nearby. Proverbs 18:24 reads (literally), "A man of friends [or neighbours/companions] comes to ruin, but there is one who loves and cleaves more than a brother". Like many proverbs, it is expressed crisply and a little cryptically. But it means something like this: *You can have many people around you with whom you have some kind of relationship. But when it comes to difficult times, these shallow so-called "friendships" won't help you much. You may still come to ruin. But there is such a thing as one who loves and cares and is more to you even than a brother.* So the Bible recognises that a neighbour—someone who just happens to be in your life—can become something more significant: someone who loves you and cares for you, and you for them. In other words, a true friend.

Friendship Building Blocks

We know in experience that at least three factors can build this kind of strong friendship. First, there is a shared history. As I grow older, I value greatly those who perhaps knew my parents while they were alive, those who watched our children grow up, those with whom I have lived through some adventures. New friendships can be wonderful. But it is hard to find a substitute for a shared history. When Paul writes from prison that Aristarchus, Mark and Jesus called Justus are "the only men of the circumcision [that is, fellow Jews] among my fellow workers for the kingdom of God", it is perhaps no surprise that he goes on to say that "they have been a comfort to me" (Colossians 4:11). There was, at the most basic level, so much shared history between them all.

Second, there can be shared interests. We naturally gravitate to those who enjoy the same sport, similar reading or viewing, comparable holidays or travel, or have overlapping tastes in music or whatever it may be.

Third—and probably most important—are shared values. Supremely, we find in a fellow believer a depth of relationship that is stronger even than with a close family member who is not in Christ. But then beyond this, we find with some, more than with others, a greater depth of shared convictions about what Christ means, the substance and wonder of his gospel, and the meaning of the Scriptures.

It is the purpose of God that we should have deep friendships, nourished perhaps by shared history and interests, fed most certainly by a commonality of values.

Some Bad Reasons to Build Friendships

Such friendships are not motivated simply by what we

hope to gain from our so-called "friends". As Proverbs 14:20 sharply observes, "A poor person is hated even by his neighbour, but there are many who love the rich" (CSB). Or, to paraphrase and expand, *There won't be many self-interested people who gravitate to a poor person to be their friend, but plenty will act as if they love a rich person because they hope some of the riches will rub off on them.* It is perhaps timely to remember this in our fifties and sixties, by which time some of our neighbours or potential "friends" may indeed have become rich or successful. It is natural to want to be associated with them, as we hope some of their success or distinction will reflect well on us. And so we invite them to our homes, rather than those who can't offer us any kudos (see further Luke 14:12).

We need to beware lest these unworthy motivations creep into our building of friendships. Besides, it can be self-defeating. If we are hanging around such people too much, they will notice and get fed up with us! As Proverbs 25:17 says, "Let your foot be seldom in your neighbour's house, lest he have his fill of you and hate you". Such a one becomes an unwelcome drain on the energies of the "friend".

Some Good Reasons to Build Healthy Friendships

I think it is fair to say that the Bible gives the following three reasons to encourage us to build healthy friendships.

1. A SHARED ENJOYMENT OF GOD'S GOODNESS

First, and simplest, it is wholesome and natural that we should share our enjoyment in God's good world with others. This, essentially, is why we tell friends about a holiday or show them our photos and videos, and why they want to listen. It is why we go to a gig or a sporting event with some friends. It is just so much more enjoyable, and our hearts overflow all the more when we can enjoy them together. When something good happens, we want to celebrate with our friends—an impulse captured in Jesus' parables of the lost sheep and the lost coin (Luke 15:6, 9). The call "rejoice with me" to our friends expresses a wholesome response to the goodness of God. Our heavenly Father gives us good gifts to enjoy (1 Timothy 6:17), and we enjoy them best with one another.

If this is true for God's gifts of common grace, it is all the more true for his gifts of salvation. When God rescued his people in the days of Esther, they celebrated with gladness and feasting and by sending gifts of food to one another (Esther 9:19, 22).

C.S. Lewis shrewdly observed that there is something intrinsically open and welcoming about a healthy friendship. Whereas the boundaries of a marriage are to be carefully guarded (Hebrews 13:4, see chapter 6), friendships are open to others, so that joys and life are shared.[7] Those of us who are married would perhaps do well to consider, in our fifties and sixties, whether the sacred boundaries of our marriages have inhibited the openness of our friendships, so that our husband or wife becomes in practice our only close friend.

---

7 *The Four Loves* (Fount Paperbacks, 1977), p. 58-59.

2. SHARED WISDOM

Second, friendship is given to us so that we may learn wisdom from one another. A wise friend will guide another in ways of righteousness, by contrast with a wicked neighbour, who leads another astray (Proverbs 12:26). A true friend will not flatter, for "a man who flatters his neighbour spreads a net for his feet" (29:5). The best and sweetest thing about a friend can be the "earnest counsel" they give us (27:9). Here is one who comes alongside, who knows me and cares for me, who wants the best for me, who gives time to ponder, to pray, to seek wisdom, and then to share his or her counsel with me. Friendship does not come much better or higher than that. In the famous metaphor of the sharpening of metals, we read that "iron sharpens iron, and one man sharpens his friend" (27:17, my translation). Our fifties and sixties may be an especially good time to develop friendships in which we both seek and offer wise counsel to our friends.

3. FELLOWSHIP THROUGH LIFE'S UPS AND DOWNS

Third, and perhaps most wonderful of all, God gives us friends that we may walk through the wilderness of this world with others by our side. The author John Bunyan captured this beautifully in *The Pilgrim's Progress*, with characters like Faithful and Great-Heart. Friends are given that we may help and support one another in time of need. At a simple level, this help is practical. In Jesus' parable, when an unexpected guest comes to our house and we have nothing with which to feed them, it is to our friend that he says we will turn (Luke 11:5). Of course it is. It was the centurion's friends who spoke to Jesus for him (Luke 7:6). A friend is there for all times of life but especially "for adversity" (Proverbs 17:17). In the pressures of his trials, Jesus Christ longed for the presence and support of his friends in the Garden of Gethsemane. One of the sharp pains of his suffering was abandonment by his friends (prophesied in Psalms 38:11 and 88:18, for example). The highest thing one friend can do for another is to lay down his life (John 15:13).

One of the most striking pictures of friendship in Scripture is that of David and Jonathan. At a time of great affliction for David (see 1 Samuel 18 – 30), Jonathan deliberately came and found David, and he "strengthened his hand in God" (16:23). What a beautiful phrase that is! In his time of trial, David is tempted to despair; he is under pressure to stop believing the covenant promises of God, given to him in his anointing by Samuel, that he will be king (1 Samuel 16). He is tempted to let go of the hand of the God who walks with him in the wilderness. And God sends Jonathan to, as it were, gently but firmly put David's hand back into the hand of God. What a friend he was! He was, in the words of the proverb, a friend who loved David at all times—a brother born to walk with David in his time of adversity.

Many of us thank God for a friend who has stood by us and walked with us through the valley of the shadow of death. This reminds us that, as life goes on, people whom we value die. Most acutely, spouses die. Our parents die.

Close friends die. Some live on into very old age, of course, and what a blessing that can be. But often they do not. So when I say, "Nourish friendships", I do intend the plural. If all your friendship is poured into just one or two friends—a husband, a wife, a dear brother or sister, one particular close friend—then we are very vulnerable to the acute loneliness which comes with bereavement. To some extent, we cannot avoid this or insure ourselves against it. Some friendships will be particularly precious and close. When they end with death, the pain is sharp and deep. But I want to encourage you to cultivate a plurality of healthy friendships. Not a multiplicity, for we do not have the relational time and energy to form many close friendships. But a reasonable plurality.

Refreshing Friendships

So, if you are persuaded that this window of life is a good time to conduct an audit of your friendships and then perhaps to do something intentional to strengthen them, how are you to set about this? The answer will of course depend much on your circumstances. But here are a few factors to bear in mind.

THE BLESSINGS OF PROXIMITY

First, geography. "Better is a neighbour [or friend] who is near than a brother who is far away" (Proverbs 27:10). The word "brother" is generally stronger than the word translated "neighbour/friend". So the point is this: you may have one who has been a close friend to you but who is now—for all manner of reasons—a long way away. Remember that there is something special about being close—that is, physically close, so that you can speak face to face in the same room. A more recent friend who now lives near to you may be able to be a better friend today even than an old friend who lives far away.

Of course, we can speak and see remotely, in ways that Solomon and other wise men in the Old Testament could not. We thank God for these technologies. But there is no substitute for being face to face. As John wrote, we want to meet face to face, and to value that even above the very best digital communication (2 John 1:12). So, while we naturally want to maintain friendships at a distance if we can, and these can be very precious, we should not forget to nurture friendships close at hand.

THE VALUE OF SHARED CONVICTIONS

Second, value highly friendships with a deep level of common belief and conviction. Choose your close friends so that you do not merely like them, but you trust them to walk with you in the path of faithfulness to Christ and the Scriptures.

HOW MANY CLOSE FRIENDS?

Third, invest intentionally in a limited number of friendships. If, like me, you have moved here and there, you will probably have met a large, perhaps overwhelming, number of people with whom you could have forged a close friendship. But you can't, simply because of the numbers and the fact that they and you live in many different places. So seek out a manageable number of friends who can be true friends with you in this window of life.

Some of us can sustain and nourish close friendships with only as many as we can count on one hand; others may be able to extend the circle. See what your lifestyle can sustain. And be prepared to take some hard decisions about those with whom you are—reluctantly—not going to deepen friendship. Many of us have significantly more people with whom we *could* have become friends than the number with whom we can actually and realistically *be* friends. If these men and women have shared history with you, so much the better. If you and they enjoy similar things, so much the more natural. But even if they don't, work at nurturing these friendships. And remember that it can be a beautiful but costly thing to extend the hand of friendship to someone whom we discern perhaps has a greater need of a friend just now than we do.

With all this in mind, prayerfully consider one or two people with whom you're going to foster—or renew—a friendship. Perhaps you could make a point of asking one or two for a meal or suggest a walk together, or some other context in which friendship can grow easily and naturally. I have found that praying regularly with two other men has been a great way of building friendship. Maybe take the time and trouble to pop in for a visit; in our digitised culture, time together in the same place can feel old-fashioned. But it really is a lot better!

And, if you find it hard to develop such nourishing friendships, in all your efforts remember this: Jesus really is the friend who sticks closer than a brother. You can rely on him.

Questions and Responses

1. Think through who your closest friends are. What makes their friendships so valuable?
2. Which of your close friends live near to where you are now?
3. When have you learned wisdom from a friend or shared wisdom with a friend? Think about how you might do this more.
4. Which friends have walked with you through sad or difficult days? Pray to be this sort of friend to others.

Ruth, aged 15, loved visiting her grandmother. Granny was 70 now. She hadn't had an easy life. Her husband had been abusive, and the marriage had ended very unhappily soon after Ruth's dad had been born. For years Granny had struggled with a degenerative disease. She didn't have much money.

But Ruth couldn't help noticing that there was a peace about Granny, a quiet contentment—something Ruth didn't see in her mum and dad or the parents of her friends. Ruth wondered why Granny, whose life was so hard, could be like this.

She couldn't fail to notice the Bible always there beside Granny's bed. She resolved to ask her next time she visited.

Conclusion

A Heart at Peace

O Lord, my heart is not lifted up;
my eyes are not raised too high;
I do not occupy myself with things
too great and too marvellous for me.
But I have calmed and quietened my soul,
like a weaned child with its mother;
like a weaned child is my soul within me.

Psalm 131:1-2

I have learned in whatever situation I am to be content. I know how to be brought low, and I know how to abound. In any and every circumstance, I have learned the secret of facing plenty and hunger, abundance and need. I can do all things through him who strengthens me.

Philippians 4:11-13

I began this book with a chapter about a godly heart. Let me close with a chapter about the quiet heart. This is one of the greatest blessings as life goes on from year to year. Let me encourage you to seek this and, by the grace of God, to grow such a spirit during this "afternoon" window of life. Not the least of the blessings will be that, if you live into old age, you will reap then the good harvest you are sowing now.

A Blessing of the Gospel

A quiet heart is a blessing of the gospel. David wrote Psalm 131, quoted above. David was the son of God, the anointed king, the prototype messiah. In Psalm 131 he tells us how he learns to have a quiet heart. He is tempted to raise his heart—to think too highly about himself and his abilities. He is tempted to raise his eyes—that is, his desires and ambitions—too high. He is tempted to be concerned about "things too great and too marvellous" for him—a shorthand for things he cannot understand and things he cannot control. Yet he renounces all proud thoughts that tell him he can understand these things, let alone control them. And so he calms and quietens his soul, and learns to rest in his covenant God like a young child with a mother, in a picture of trusting calm.

In writing this psalm, David foreshadows the Lord Jesus, the true Son of God from all eternity, as he renounces all temptations to proud independence from his Father, and learns to rest and to trust. In the midst of troubles and trials—indeed in the midst of a troubled heart (e.g. John 12:27, echoing several psalms)—Jesus learns a quiet heart of trust. He learns in his life on earth what it is to entrust himself to his Father (1 Peter 2:23).

For those who belong to Jesus Christ, a quiet heart is therefore a privilege of the gospel. Paul speaks of it as a contentment that needs to be learned. As we grow older, we have great need of a quiet and contented heart, for there will be many things we can neither control or comprehend. Without Christ, these things will make us troubled, anxious and discontented. We will become grumblers, full of self-pity, or those who grieve without hope. But in Christ we may gradually learn the blessings of a quiet heart. We know that God understands all that we cannot comprehend and controls all that lies outside our frustrating limits. He weaves his fathomless wisdom in a way that is utterly beyond us—and he does so for his glory and our good. In this assurance, our hearts can rest.

I want to consider four threats to a quiet heart as we look back to the past and two dangers as we move into the future.

Threats to a Quiet Heart Arising from the Past

PAST HURTS UNFORGIVEN

It is a frightening experience to discover that some hurt done to you, perhaps deep in the past, is still exercising a poisonous power over your heart. Years ago, someone—a family member, a work colleague, a neighbour, a member of your church, a friend—behaved badly towards you. They hurt you. In time, you offered them forgiveness. Perhaps they asked for forgiveness and were so grateful when you and they were reconciled. Perhaps they never asked for it, and the relationship remained unrepaired—but, so far as you are concerned, that forgiveness was offered, and you had moved on. You thought it was over: done, covered, cleared, cleansed. The boil was lanced; the wound was healing.

But now, years later, you find in your heart a lingering resentment—a root of bitterness that spews out poison into your inner being. What then? Say there isn't scope still for profitable conversation with the person concerned. Indeed, they may by now be far away; they may even have died. What then is to be done in your own heart? You cannot have a quiet heart while bitter resentment is leaking into its recesses.

The answer is the same as it was when you first faced this challenge to the spirit: you need to feel afresh how much the Lord has forgiven you. "As the Lord has forgiven you," writes the apostle Paul, "so you also must forgive" (Colossians 3:13). The logic of this is powerfully unfolded in Jesus' story of the unforgiving servant (Matthew 18:21-35). In the second half of the story, we learn that the servant is owed "a hundred denarii" by a fellow servant, which is between a quarter and a third of a year's pay for a working man (see Matthew 20:2); it is a not insignificant sum and represents a hurt that may be deep and painful. The point of the story is not that this debt is small in absolute terms but rather that it is minuscule by comparison with the debt that the first servant himself has just been forgiven by his master, the king: a debt of 10,000 talents. A few years before the time of Jesus, the total annual revenue of Judea was about 600 talents.[8] The amount this servant owes the king is well more than the total money in circulation in the whole country at the time. "Ten thousand" was the biggest number in the Greek language; and the talent was the biggest unit of currency. So, we might say, he owed the king trillions of pounds, dollars or euros. What he has been forgiven is astronomical. And yet the servant will not forgive his fellow servant an infinitesimally smaller debt, and is condemned for his unforgiveness.

What you and I needed when first we were wronged was this gospel: that the Lord has forgiven me an astronomical debt, far bigger than I could have paid in many lifetimes. I needed my eyes opened to the enormity of my own sin. Then and only then were the padlocks of my heart unfastened to offer forgiveness to another man or woman.

But the depths of self-deception are such that I may think I have forgiven when in fact there is some poisonous residue of bitterness left uncleansed. The medicine now is the same as the medicine at the beginning. But it must be reapplied. You may have been so terribly hurt, perhaps by abuse or infidelity, that you understandably struggle to forgive. I do not mean to minimise this at all. This may be a time to speak—or speak again—to a pastor or counsellor about it. These things are not healed easily. But, whoever you are, let me exhort you: whenever you find some trace of unresolved bitterness in your heart, don't let it fester; take it to the Lord and ask

8 Josephus, *Antiquities* 17.320.

for his help. Pray and ponder your own depravity afresh. And then, as your heart is filled again with wonder at what the Lord has forgiven you, bring this past hurt into the light of the Lord's forgiving love for you.

REGRETS FOR PAST CHOICES

By the time you reach your fifties or sixties, you will have come to quite a few forks in the road. At each such fork you will have chosen one path and not the other. Some of these will be of massive significance. You may have chosen to marry (or not to marry) a particular person (or perhaps they chose not to marry you). Perhaps you opted to move to a different country. There will have been choices about the care of an ageing parent. You will have decided how to respond to a situation in the family. Maybe you decided to take, or to not take, a job that was offered.

And now you may look back and regret one choice or another. "I wish I hadn't decided to marry him." "How I long to turn the clock back and choose again what to say in that crisis." "If only I had gone the other way." The road not taken now seems full of hope and promise, when the path you took turned into a miry misery.

So what do you do? You will most certainly not have a quiet heart with thoughts like these raging around within you. "If only" is a phrase that grows louder as it echoes in a troubled heart. There is only one place to turn, and that is to the God who stands outside of time. Every single one of the days that were formed for you were written in God's book of wisdom and love before you were even conceived (Psalm 139:16). He has watched; he has guided; he has led. At every fork where you made a choice, his unseen hand has been with you. We make many mistakes, but God never makes mistakes. He weaves our mistakes into his tapestry of loving beauty.

So, just as a young person will be very wary of risk (especially in our risk-averse cultures) unless she believes that God watches over her, so a middle-aged person will sing the "if only" song on repeat unless she truly grasps that we live our lives under the watchful guiding eye of the covenant God who loved us from eternity past and will guide and lead us to eternity future. And so we may pray with sober realism, "Lord God, I do wish I had chosen differently about this. It does seem to me that it would have been better. But I bow before your unfathomable wisdom."

It may help to say or to sing William Cowper's great hymn:

God moves in a mysterious way,
His wonders to perform;
He plants his footsteps in the sea
And rides upon the storm.

Deep in unfathomable mines
Of never-failing skill,
He treasures up his bright designs
And works his sovereign will …

Judge not the Lord by feeble sense,
But trust him for his grace;

Behind a frowning providence,
He hides a smiling face.

DISAPPOINTMENT WITH PAST FAILURES

Very few reach their later decades without some lingering sense of disappointment. The realisation that I am not going to change the world can be hard to bear after the hopefulness of early adulthood.

I suppose that sport is the arena in which this is felt soonest. When someone much younger than you plays in the Premier League or the World Series, or wins Wimbledon or the Masters, it dawns on you—you who were such a promising young athlete—that you will never win the glittering prizes of which you dreamed. You watch an Olympian who comes fourth, say, in their post-race interview: "I am sure one day I will win the medal I dream of". You do not need to be a grumpy old man to think to yourself, "Hang on a minute. How can you possibly be sure?"

Most of us had hopes in our careers that have not been fulfilled. When we were young, we had thought that one day we'd make it to CEO or go right to the top of our profession, or make some other significant mark on the world. These hopes are sometimes fuelled by belonging to families in which ancestors or siblings have had such success. Yet as you move through middle age and out the other side, gradually it dawns on you that you will never make it beyond some rather modest level of success. Perhaps there is also a lingering sense that you deserved better than you got—that some discrimination or injustice has barred you from rising as high as your talents deserve. But, one way or another, you feel disappointed in yourself. You simply haven't achieved what you had hoped to achieve.

So what are you to do with this disappointment? Part of the medicine is the same as for the regrets about past choices (above): simply to trust that God, in his unfathomable wisdom and love, has your days in his book. But you may also be helped by another thought, and it is this: there will be many surprises on the last day about what truly counts as success. The great gospel principle that "the last will be first and the first last" warns us not to be too sure that we know what success means (Matthew 20:16).

I think it was the 20th-century archbishop William Temple who compared our cultures to a shop window in which the price tags have all been muddled up and switched around—so that things of immense value are labelled as cheap, and worthless stuff is sold for a fortune. It's a good picture. The world places its high-price labels on worldly success. It measures achievement by criteria which God does not share (to put it mildly). The man who has been a faithful husband, a caring father, a conscientious worker and a kind friend may just find that in God's sight his life has been a lot more successful than a man who has all the markers of outward success. The man or woman who has learned contentment in being unmarried and has developed kind and godly friendships, or the wife and mother who has patiently cared for her children and achieved little in the eyes of a muddled world, may find that they are highly esteemed in God's sight. So, part of the remedy for disappointment with past failures is simply to re-evaluate what counts as success or failure. May we be those who see as God sees.

SADNESS WITH FAMILY UNBELIEF

I want to mention one further threat to a quiet heart, not only because this threatens me but also because I keep meeting men and women who carry around with them the same thing: a lasting sadness from family unbelief. By the time we reach our fifties or sixties, these sorrows can seem to be hard-wired into our lives. The grief caused by a close family member—perhaps especially a son or daughter—who turns from following Jesus or repeatedly resists the offer of the gospel is often one of the sharpest and most agonising griefs for a believer in the afternoon of life. When this loved one persists in living in the far country, it feels so hard to go on praying, day by day, that God will give them repentance that leads to life. How many of God's "bottles" are filled with the tears of mums and dads for an unbelieving daughter or a son far from the loving Saviour (Psalm 56:8).

How are such tears, and the daily prayers that accompany them, to be held together with a contented and quiet heart? Not—most certainly not—by a quiet fatalism that stops us interceding. For we are taught by the Lord Jesus to pray and not to lose heart (Luke 18:1). We are to pray day by day and to grieve for such unbelief. And yet, most wonderfully, such prayers may be prayed, and these tears can be shed, from a heart that is quiet before God. It is possible to cast these anxieties and cares upon the Lord, knowing that we matter to him (1 Peter 5:7). It is possible to learn contentment as we cast our unbelieving family members onto the Lord's grace, trusting that our prayers may be answered after we ourselves have been taken to glory. The work of conversion really is the work of God. No son or daughter has ever been saved by good parenting, and no one upon whom God has set his love will ever miss out on God's blessing through imperfect parenting. We are very prone to beat ourselves over the head and wish we had been better parents (or better children, husbands, wives, brothers, sisters, uncles, aunts, grandparents or whatever). Probably we could and should have been. But the mercy of God does not depend upon us.

Dangers for a Quiet Heart as We Face the Future

PREPARATION FOR FUTURE BEREAVEMENTS

Bereavement can come at any time of life. But in our fifties and sixties, we begin to be aware that among our peers, the deaths of a precious wife or husband, of dear parents, even of a young adult son or daughter, are a lot more common than they were when we were younger. We find ourselves going to such funerals. We watch a friend of about our age going through such tear-stained sorrow. And we are foolish if we do not recognise that this could come to us. For some of us it will. Perhaps it already has.

Each of us does well to consider this and to prepare for bereavement. Anxiety about terrible things that might happen—and they might—can become a crippling slavery if we do not apply the gospel of Christ to our fears (see Psalm 112:7-8). A heart that is constantly worrying about what happens if a loved one is taken from us will struggle to be at peace. This may happen. It could happen any day. We know this.

How then are we to keep a quiet heart in the face of such sober realism? The answer is to hope in Christ, and to hope in a way that our this-life-obsessed cultures can never do. Let us keep the focus of our prayers on new life in Christ even more than on healing in this age, as wonderful as that is. Let us keep one another looking up to Christ, rehearsing what he has done for us in the forgiveness of our sins, reminding one another of his promises of bodily resurrection and the life of the age to come. That will not stop bereavement being desperately painful as we face a future without this dearly loved companion. But it can help us keep a quiet and trusting heart day by day as we face these otherwise paralysing possibilities. For we may know that God's grace in Jesus really is sufficient and that our Good Shepherd really will walk with us through the darkest valley.

BEWILDERMENT AT CHANGING CULTURE

It is not wise to say that the old days were better than today (Ecclesiastes 7:10). And yet this is precisely what begins to enter our conversations from our fifties onwards. Before that there were not really any "old days" to speak of; but now that there are, we defend ourselves against change through bouts of nostalgia. Perhaps at the moment this is a peculiarly pressing problem, since Western cultures seem to be shifting at dizzying speeds. And I know from my own experience how disorienting this can be. And all this can introduce turmoil into an otherwise quiet heart, as though my peaceful pond is invaded by wild breakers from outside—and so I conjure in my imagination the quiet waters of an idyllic past age.

When changing culture confuses me, or when I do not understand my children or grandchildren—when I, perhaps rightly, realise that they inhabit a thought-world significantly different from my own—how am I to keep a quiet heart? I take it that the answer—as to every other challenge—is the gospel, and the gospel understood as God's power to save in *any* culture. I need to be realistic and to face the fact that the culture of my childhood or young adulthood was just as wicked as the culture today. It was just that it was wicked in different ways—ones to which I was blind.

In our context of sexual chaos, I often remind myself that the Corinth in which the apostle Paul ministered was a terrible place. It was the kind of city where a man could sleep with and live with his stepmother and a church could approve of him (1 Corinthians 5:1). It is hard to imagine that anything we face today could be worse. And yet the gospel of God's grace saved some and brought into existence a church of Christ—and neither Paul nor his Lord gave up on them.

We need to remind one another both of the depravity of every culture and the power of God in the gospel. Confident in the gospel—and the God of the gospel—we can walk through these days with a quiet and trusting heart.

Laying Deep Foundations

I want to encourage you, as you travel through your fifties and sixties, to cultivate a quiet heart, to learn contentment, to believe the gospel of God's grace and to apply that gospel specifically to these threats and dangers, and perhaps others. The prize is of great value. It is a wonderful thing to walk through troubles and changes with a settled habit of entrusting yourself to the God who loves you and walks with you through Jesus. Seek to learn this in the afternoon of life so that—if God spares you for the "evening"—you may enjoy this blessing until the day you die or Jesus returns, which is better still. How deeply wonderful to lay the foundations, in our fifties and sixties, for the beautiful contentment that Ruth saw in her granny in my example at the start of the chapter. You are not old, not young and not done in that endeavour. Time spent meditating on the sufficiency of God and the unbeatable adequacy of Jesus' grace is never time wasted!

Questions and Responses

1. Would it be true to say that you—by and large—have a quiet heart as in Psalm 131? If not, what are the main reasons why you don't?

2. Is there some bitterness or resentment lurking in your heart? Talk about it with a close friend or pastor. And then ask God to show you afresh how much the Lord has forgiven you.

3. What regrets do you have about past choices or failures? What would it look like to seek a renewed trust in the Lord's kind and sovereign wisdom over your life?

4. Entrust unbelieving family members to God's mercy day by day; weep for them, but then learn to leave them before the throne of grace. You may find it helpful to do this with a partner in prayer.

5. Think with those dearest to you about the fact that one day bereavement will strike you or them. Maybe talk about this in groups of friends. Face this before God. Entrust them, and let them entrust you, to God's wise loving kindness.

6. What changes in our culture are you troubled by? And what specifically may have been not so good about the "good old days"? If there are believers among younger friends or family members, perhaps you can talk these things over with them.

Lola feels exhausted. She's 52, and she's got as little energy as she had when she was pregnant 25 years ago. Every night, she rolls over to go to sleep knowing she'll be awake a couple of hours later, sweaty and uncomfortable, her mind racing with what the next day holds at work or thoughts about her grown children's troubles. Her tiredness and the incessant hot flushes she's now experiencing mean that she's grumpy a lot of the time. Lola joins in with her moaning colleagues—something she'd have resisted a few years ago.

"Why bother being different?" she secretly thinks. "The menopause is so unfair; surely I deserve a break after all these years of trying so hard to be the good Christian?"

Appendix

A Godly Menopause

BY SARAH ALLEN

If you're in the target age group for this book and are female, then you most likely have felt the effects of the menopause. If you're male and in the same age bracket, then women you care about—a wife, sister, friends or colleagues—will be going through these changes. The menopause is inescapable! Until relatively recently, however, it's been a no-go subject for public conversation, perhaps especially in the church.

So, I need first to explain a few key terms which will crop up in these pages as I explore how Christians can understand this dimension of mid-life and live well amid its challenges.

"Menopause" itself refers to the ending of monthly periods caused by the reduction of oestrogen produced by a woman's ovaries. The few years leading up to this point, when symptoms of this hormonal change may first appear, is referred to as perimenopause. These experiences, such as hot flushes, erratic and sometimes much heavier periods, sleeplessness, mood swings and brain fog, can also carry on beyond menopause for some few years. A year after her last period, a woman is said to be post-menopausal.

You can see from this description that menopause is a completely normal and natural process, though not necessarily easy. The level of symptoms and the age at which it happens vary considerably, though the average age of menopause in the West is 51, and most women experience moderate discomfort. There are those, of course, who sail through this time of life barely noticing any changes, and others whose lives are significantly disrupted.

The Secular Story

The variability of symptoms and their severity might be a surprise to you if you've been paying attention to today's media experts and the celebrities who publish books and front documentaries. Most of them suggest that menopausal changes are something to be feared and so to be resisted, whether through diet, exercise or, most often, medication (hormone replacement therapy, or HRT).

It *is* good that now (at last!) women are taken more seriously by their employers and family doctors and are less likely to be dismissed or misdiagnosed. And these books do supply some helpful practical and scientific content. But it is *not* good if menopause is presented as a time of inevitable distress or as an obstacle for women to overcome. Worse still is the idea that orientation towards myself will solve my problems.

Scratch the surface of these menopause guides and we often find idols of career success, youthful looks and health. They make minimising suffering and maximising self-satisfaction their primary aim; their message is "Look young, feel young, and focus on yourself".

And if these are your driving motivations, then the difficulties of menopause—the tiredness and brain fog, ageing skin and joints, sleep-disruption and embarrassing hot flushes—can feel devastating.

So, it shouldn't be a surprise that emotional distress can be a significant part of modern menopause. Not only are hormones affecting our moods, but we are facing the practical pressures of middle age. We're also seeing and feeling the ageing of our bodies at a time when such limitations are something to be feared. Menopause can act like a spoon, stirring all these troubles together and, in doing so, stirring up our sinful desires to complain or despair.

The Bible's Better Help

Understanding the biological mechanisms at work in our bodies as we go through what previous generations called "the change" is a great help. Demystifying experiences can give us a sense of relief. We can think, "This is normal; it will pass" when the hot flushes keep on coming. But we shouldn't stop there. The Bible gives us an additional framework for understanding our bodies and their weaknesses which can give us more than relief. It can help us see a purpose in the menopause and even lead us to joy in the changes.

YOUR BODY IS A GIFT

The contemporary Western world tells you that your body belongs to you. You have control over it and can decide what happens to it, from how you have your hair cut to who you sleep with. So, when signs of ageing arise, we're quick to try to think of choices we can make to take back control and to limit the loss of a carefully cultivated identity.

The very first chapters of the Bible argue against this belief. In Genesis 1 and 2 we are told that our bodies are created after God's pattern. He says, "Let us make man in our image, after our likeness" (Genesis 1:26). Just as any piece of art belongs to its creator, so we, body and soul, belong to him.

Christopher has clearly explained in chapter 2 how our bodies are dead because of sin. They are crumbling and decaying, and no exercise regime or dosage of HRT will reverse this. Menopause is evidence of this unavoidable reality and underlines the fact that we are not our own. Our bodies are running on God's timetable, heading towards death.

So, it is good to look after our bodies because they are his created gift, but not for some foolish idea that we can stay young for ever, always able to think and run as fast as we did when we were 35. We exercise and take medication to honour the generosity of God in entrusting creation to us.

And we cling on to a second truth. We doubly belong to God because he has redeemed us for himself. 1 Corinthians 6:19-20 makes it plain: "You are not your own, for you were bought with a price", so you must therefore "glorify God in your body". The payment of Christ's death was not to purchase disembodied souls for his Father but to win people, each with a body and soul. Our menopausal bodies are his precious possession.

God does not reject lined faces or greying hair as ugly or unfitting for his kingdom, though we might struggle at the sight of ourselves in the mirror. In fact, in Proverbs 16:31, God tells us that grey hair is a "crown of glory" when achieved through a "righteous life". It is in our bodies that he wants us to act out the reality of his gospel. Our righteousness is gifted to us when we are purchased by him and is seen when, with hands, feet, brains and lips, we live and work for him.

Living this way, the visible changes in our body are not something to hide but something to celebrate for they speak of years of faithfulness. The signs of age that come with menopause signify the Lord's faithfulness to us and our faithful walk with him. We need a radical reorientation away from our culture's preoccupation with outward appearance. Our challenge is to look in the mirror and say thank you to our sustaining, providing God. Rather than an initial shock when we see yet again that we are not 40, or even 50, and despair at what we've lost, we can discipline our thoughts to recall all he has done to bring us to this point and to reflect on the purpose of it all.

ITS PURPOSE IS FRUITFULNESS

Turning away from the self-preoccupation with how we look or feel and turning towards our master is a battle—but it brings peace. And it causes us to remember his plan. Back in Genesis 1, as we are told about our creation in God's image, we hear a double command. God's images are to multiply and to rule, following the pattern that God himself began as he brought order out of chaos and filled it in the creation.

Eve, in the next couple of chapters, is particularly associated with this task of procreating. Her name means "life", because she would be "the mother of all living" (3:20). So central was Eve's motherly calling that it was this area of her life which was particularly blighted after the Fall; she would experience "pain in childbearing" (3:16). It is no wonder then that Eve's daughters suffer not only in childbirth but in all aspects of their fertility—from endometriosis to infertility to menopause. Women are called to fruitfulness, but their calling is made very hard.

When our periods come to an end, we know there will be no more children. For some mothers this is sad, though the "delightful burden" of parenting carries on;[9] for those who have longed to be mothers but haven't had children, it can be far more painful. Yet this ending of biological fruitfulness is also a gift, strange as that may seem.

---

9 I heard this memorable description of parenting from Ann Benton.

It is a gift because it is an opportunity to realise the two-fold calling we have. Just as God possesses our bodies twice over, so he has given us two purposes. Some of us may never be able to fulfil our bodily potential for fruitfulness; but all of us can live out our calling to spiritual fruitfulness: to be part of the calling that all God's redeemed people have, to "go … and make disciples" (Matthew 28:19) and to nurture new life in many ways.

It's tempting, though, to get comfortable in our ways or to be over-awed by those younger women around us who might seem more energetic or more confident. Perhaps you've been hurt by people in your church, or you feel that you've tried to help others, and it hasn't worked out. Maybe, like Lola, you are just tired out and disheartened by the lack of spiritual fruit among your non-Christian friends. Better, you may think, to invest in your biological family, who, after all, do need you. Or to concentrate on nurturing your few close friends with whom you feel safe.

But fruitfulness *is* painful. Jesus talked of himself as a seed which must die in order to bear much fruit. Just as biological childbearing involves blood and pain, "spiritual childbearing" is painful too. There will be no fruit without loss and sacrifice. There will be no Christian joy without self-giving.

Don't use menopause as a reason to withdraw from Christian service. Use it as a reason to get involved, to do something new and to take a risk for fruitfulness. And make this the main reason to get medical help for your physical struggles or to make necessary adjustments to your lifestyle—this shouldn't be just about being more comfortable but about equipping ourselves to be more fruitful, whether that is talking with our neighbours about Jesus or leading a Bible study or getting involved with a youth group or starting up a new outreach opportunity.

The Spiritual Strength You Need

Perhaps that all sounds a bit glib and all too easy. Your situation may be especially complicated, and you may have heard exhortations like that too many times. Perhaps you are weary and not feeling well at all—physically or spiritually.

The Lord knows.

And his word speaks wisdom into the turbulence experienced by some at menopause. This stage of life is not unknown to God, nor is he indifferent to his people's struggles. Hebrews reminds us that Christ knows what it is like to have a body; he was "fully human in every way" (2:17, NIV). And while he didn't make it to middle age, nor did he experience the troubles of female life, Jesus did suffer in his body. He is a "merciful and faithful high priest" (v 17), who is able to "sympathize with our weaknesses", who can provide us with "mercy and … grace to help in time of need" (4:15-16).

These weaknesses, we find, are about more than the agony of fibroids or the distress of extreme mood swings or the exhaustion brought about by night sweats. The mercy and grace that Jesus provides for us is power and presence when our physical weakness leads to spiritual weakness. It is at these times that we are tempted to doubt God's goodness or to pity ourselves and envy others or to indulge ourselves in angry outbursts. The troubles of menopause can become a route away from life in Christ, or they can become a pathway to more joyful dependence on him. He prays for us; will we come to him?

Menopausal women, those women "of a certain age", are sometimes mocked for being "difficult". This is blamed, patronisingly, on hormones. The stereotype is of a woman who complains, gets angry and makes a fuss—at work, in a shop or even in the church. Perhaps there is a grain of truth in it all. Hormonal change can make us more irritable. And life experience can make us grumpy too. We get angry with injustice and unfairness, as well as at the petty annoyances all around.

This is our challenge—to scrutinise the rising tide of frustration we feel and bring it before our Lord. Confessing our unrighteous anger, we should then ask if there is something we *should* be angry or upset about? Is there some cause we should be fighting for? And if there is, can we, with the Lord's mercy and grace, bring fruit out of the pain? Rather than letting out the throttle of our anger, we need to seek his grace, read his word and then speak our words in his strength.

A secular book on female middle age was released a few years ago called *Hagitude.* It relied on New Age ideas and paganism to argue that women should embrace their menopausal and post-menopausal changes and become the powerful, wise women of myth.

It's true that middle-aged women have the potential for a special kind of power. As our hormones reduce, our life experiences grow—and in the hand of God, this can be used with great effect. Again and again in the pages of Scripture, and in church history, women who have gone through the change are held up as examples. Not of some magical power but of God's grace. Menopause isn't a curse, whatever Lola thinks. It is God's gift to us, that we might become more and more fruitful as we remain in him, relying on his strength alone.

Sarah Allen is the author of *Pause: How to Enjoy God, Find Hope and Bear Fruit Through Midlife and Menopause* (10Publishing, 2024); and *Clothed with Strength: Women Who Built the Church and Changed the World* (10Publishing, 2023); and co-author of *Resilient Faith: Learning to Rely on Jesus in the Struggles of Life* (Crossway, 2023).

Acknowledgements

The idea for this short pastoral book emerged in conversations with Alison Mitchell at The Good Book Company some years ago. I am grateful to her for stirring me up to pursue this, and then to Carl Laferton for his encouragement and ideas, and to Rachel Jones, my wise and unfailingly encouraging editor. Together with their colleagues at The Good Book Company, they have contributed perhaps more than they realise to the completion of the book.

In addition, I owe a debt of gratitude to a number of pastors who have kindly contributed their pastoral wisdom at various times in the writing. I am especially grateful to Doug McCallum, my minister at Cambridge Presbyterian Church. Others who have read parts or all of the manuscript and passed on helpful comments include Nick Alexander, Alistair Begg, Piers Bickersteth, Richard Coombs, Matt Fuller, Jonathan Griffiths, Rob Hudson, David Jackman, Paul Levy, Simon Manchester and Alasdair Paine.

Several couples—too many to name—in or beyond their fifties and sixties have contributed without realising it, by their often shining examples of Christ-likeness. Most of these have been at Tyndale House, St Andrew the Great Church or Cambridge Presbyterian Church.

Most of all, I want to thank my wife, Carolyn—herself still in this window of life—who has walked with me through these decades, and now beyond into my seventies. Her love, her prayers and her example mean more to me than I can say.

Christopher Ash

Christopher Ash

Remaking

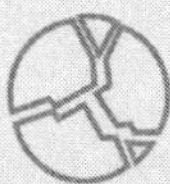

a broken

world

The heart of the Bible story

thegoodbook.com | thegoodbook.co.uk
thegoodbook.com.au | thegoodbook.co.nz

BIBLICAL | RELEVANT | ACCESSIBLE

At The Good Book Company we are dedicated to helping Christians and local churches grow. We believe that God's growth process always starts with hearing clearly what he has said to us through his timeless and flawless word—the Bible.

Ever since we opened our doors in 1991, we have been striving to produce resources that are biblical, relevant, and accessible. By God's grace, we have grown to become an international publisher, encouraging ordinary Christians of every age and stage and every background and denomination to live for Christ day by day and equipping churches to grow in their knowledge of God, their love for one another, and the effectiveness of their outreach.

Call one of our friendly team for a discussion of your needs or visit one of our local websites for more information on the resources and services we provide.

Your friends at The Good Book Company